THE DOUBLE BED BOOK

THE DOUBLE BED BOOK

Sandra Harris

Q

QUARTET BOOKS

LONDON   MELBOURNE   NEW YORK

First published by Quartet Books Limited 1984
A member of the Namara Group
27/29 Goodge Street, London W1P 1FD

Copyright © 1984 by Sandra Harris
Line illustrations copyright © Sandra Harris 1984
All other illustrations as credited

British Library Cataloguing in Publication Data

Harris, Sandra, *1942–*
 The double bed book.
 1. Beds and bedsteads—Social aspects
 —Anecdotes, facetiae, satire, etc.
 I. Title
 392'.36   GT450

ISBN 0-7043-3479-8

Designed by Namara Features Limited
Typeset by MC Typeset, Chatham, Kent
Printed and bound in Great Britain by
Mackays of Chatham Ltd, Kent

CONTENTS

Dedication
To Vivienne Shuster, who has all the best ideas

Author's Acknowledgements
The author's thanks to Angie Pearce Barker, Keith Kyle, Adrienne Brown, Desley Deike, Philip Jenkinson and Winston Churchill MP

The Importance of Being a Double Bed, An Introduction

'Item. I give unto my wife my second-best bed, with the furniture.'

W. SHAKESPEARE (WILL 25 MARCH 1616)

WAS THERE EVER a statement that underlined the true importance of the double bed more than this? Mr and Mrs Shakespeare of Stratford may, contrary to popular legend, have led a blameless and fulfilled married life but I shall never believe they were as one in bed. That she merited only the second-best bed speaks volumes for Mistress Anne: she was probably loyal, certainly dutiful, but sexy? Never; not in the second-best bed.

A double bed is not merely a piece of furniture chosen along with the chairs, tables and carpets. There is something mystical about the double bed that immediately elevates it to another plane. As it sits solidly in the master bedroom of a family of substance it is the core of the house, its very centre. It is where the children of the household are conceived and possibly where they are born. When they are ill or need to be pampered they are allowed in the double bed, surrounded by potions and bedding and importance. As they turn into young adolescents the same double bed that nourished and cosseted them becomes embarrassing in its fecundity. How horrifying and disgusting to have such solid proof that their parents still 'do it'. If the bed should creak on occasion, not in protest but in celebration, how appalling! And yet when those same adolescents turn into ordinary people again and set up on their own the choice of single or double bed is of major importance.

A single bed is a bed for sleep. A double bed is a statement of intent. Single people who swear their double beds are strictly for comfort will never be totally believed. Even when they argue, quite truthfully, that sex is just one of the pleasures a double bed can offer, the fact of its existence points to a sybaritic owner, ever on the lookout for the good things in life. Just by being there a double bed suggests body warmth and a private

sexuality all its own. Even a respectable bed with its legs covered in candlewick has an aura of hedonism, while glimpsing an unmade double bed in the morning half-light is like catching a girl in her camiknickers. There is absolutely nothing wrong in it but it is naughty nevertheless.

Twenty years or so ago the implications of a double bed were far more serious. The moral indignation that erupted throughout the British Isles when HRH Princess Margaret demanded that the twin beds on the royal yacht, *Britannia*, be swapped for a double during her honeymoon with Tony Armstrong-Jones could be heard from John o'Groats to Land's End. It was not that anyone *minded* exactly – they would be married after all – but it did not seem properly royal somehow, which just goes to show that Victorian morals may look dead but they are not lying down. We claim to like our royal family to show that they are human but we do not want them to spell it out, and that is what double beds do. They state their intentions – honourable or not.

They also exercise an endless fascination, and so it comes as no surprise to find that the greatest tourist attraction of London's Victoria and Albert Museum is the Great Bed of Ware. It is awesome. Just thinking about what must have gone on in that vastness defies even the most fertile imagination. After all this is a bed which measures ten feet seven inches by ten feet ten inches and is over seven feet high. Historians argue over its precise age, but Shakespeare certainly knew about it and mentioned it in *Twelfth Night* (1601). When Sir Toby Belch advises Sir Andrew Aguecheek to pen a challenge to his supposed rival, he suggests putting as many lies in a sheet of paper as will lie in it, 'although the sheet were big enough for the bed of Ware in England'.

It is intriguing to compare the Great Bed of Ware to other beds of similar vintage with historical associations. They are tiny – generally short and squat – no matter how impressive and grand their carvings and tapestries. I shall never forget the deep disappointment I felt when I first gazed at Henry VIII's bed at Hampton Court. It is certainly a double bed but of such an insignificant size. Can this really be where not only Queen Elizabeth I but also the entire Church of England were conceived? History does not reveal any important or royal conceptions in the Great Bed of Ware but at the inn where it was installed, the Saracen's Head in the town of Ware, Hertfordshire, it did terrific business. People would travel from far and wide to try it out, and the room where it rested was often let out to a

The Great Bed of Ware *c.* 1590: VICTORIA AND ALBERT MUSEUM, LONDON

dozen or so people at a time. It also had a ghost. The bedmaker, Jonas Fosbrooke, who was originally responsible for the bed, was said to haunt it, jealously pinching and scratching those brave enough to share it. Few were put off by a mere ghost, however, and for those interested in truly splendid seduction there was no better place than under the highly experienced canopy of the Great Bed of Ware.

Therein lies the fascination for true double-bed connoisseurs. When they find *the* bed that is the most extraordinary, the most amazing, the most seductive, it is not size or magnificence of adornment but atmosphere that matters. Another bed that would satisfy most sensation-seekers was designed for an Indian maharajah. It was built out of solid silver and although not over-large is the best example of genuine kitsch that I have been able to find for this book. It is possible to describe it as a four-poster, but each post is a life-size, life-coloured statue of a woman with painted enamel eyes and real hair. Secreted under the mattress of this work of art is a music box so that when the great man lay down, his weight started the music playing and triggered the clockwork system that brought the statues to life. They moved the fly whisks and fans in their hands rhythmically in time to the music. It was said that the maharajah was so fond of this bed he wanted to take it with him whenever he travelled on tiger shoots and so forth. This idea was sadly abandoned when it was discovered that the bed weighed over a ton.

The maharajah's bed could only have been designed for one man. The most famous and outrageous double bed ever made was planned to accommodate a multitude. It was actually designed by a certain Doctor Graham, who called it the 'celestial bed', and it was quite simply extraordinary. Vast — twelve feet long by nine feet wide — it was described in loving detail by the good doctor himself:

> The celestial bed rests on six massive and transparent columns, coverings of purple and curtains of celestial blue surround it and the bed clothes are perfumed with the most costly essences of Arabia: it is exactly similar to those that adorn the palaces in Persia and to that of the favourite sultana in the seraglio of the Grand Turk . . . I have omitted none of the precautions which decency and delicacy have a right to exact. Neither I nor any of my people are entitled to ask who are the persons that rest in this chamber which I have denominated the Holy of Holies . . .

So sacred was the 'Holy of Holies' that the privilege of using it cost an anxious couple £50 a night when the doctor first introduced it as a cure for impotence and sterility. He rapidly increased the fee to £500 a night because of its unprecedented popularity. Whether it actually produced the desired effect is unrecorded, but it must have been great fun for those who tried it. The mattress was filled with herbs and rose petals and spices from the East. Music would issue forth from the magnificent pillars and the sheets were said to be fashioned from satin as soft as a lady's cheek.

The *piece de résistance* of the celestial bed, however, was considered to be its demonstrations, tastefully and discreetly enacted by a certain Emma Lyon. Miss Lyon, a one-time servant, would be revealed (lightly veiled or not veiled at all, depending on her mood) on and around the bed to give

Bedstead of wood decorated with black and gold lacquer in the Chinese style,
1755–60: probably Thomas Chippendale. Victoria and Albert Museum,
London. CoID PHOTOGRAPH

potential users an idea of what could be performed within its embrace. Miss Lyon was severely criticized by some writers of the day, who found her part in Doctor Graham's rituals absurd and offensive. Others were to disagree. She went on to call herself Miss Hart and then married Britain's Ambassador to Italy. As Lady Hamilton, it was not long before she was decorating the bed of one of England's most favoured heroes, Lord Nelson. How titillating to think she may have learned her craft in the silken splendour of the celestial bed.

It is a hard act to follow but many have tried and some have almost succeeded. Probably the most famous double bed of modern times is the one owned by Playboy-in-Chief, Hugh Hefner. Mr Hefner was not the first man to have an elliptical double bed (Sheraton designed that in the eighteenth century) but his is certainly the most famous. It rested, if that is the right word, in his suite in the Playboy mansion in Chicago and was fitted with every possible electronic device. At the flick of a switch 'Hef' could spin his bed a full circle and back again. He could make it shake and vibrate. Secreted behind walls of two-way mirrors was a television camera tuned into the screens dotted around the room so that, should he so desire, Hef could record the goings on in his fantasy bed and enjoy instant playback. (His favourite trick was to get his playmates to massage him all over with baby oil. 'The trouble was,' one complained, 'it got just all over everything — in our hair, our ears, and our finger-nails and you should have seen the state of those sheets . . . even though they were changed at least twice a day . . . the mess!')

Hef also had a water bed installed in his Roman-style bathroom, which lurched and heaved as if it had a life of its own. In *Big Bunny*, his private jet, he had another round bed, which matched the one he had at home almost exactly in electronic detail except that this one also featured a light box so that he could do a little work and study the photographic transparencies of future 'Playmates of the Month' from the luxury of his bed. Sadly, *Big Bunny* (and therefore the bed) was somewhat underused. Hef rarely left his Playboy mansion. During his twenty-year reign of Fantasy Land for Ageing Schoolboys he only once walked in the street. He never took a bus and never entered a shop. His wardrobe consisted almost entirely of pyjamas, and during the swinging, magical sixties when the permissive society was flaunting itself all over the Western world the man who could legitimately claim to be one of its prophets kept in touch by video.

Today those bunny girls have folded up their ears and packed away their tails. Even Hugh Hefner started to think they looked just a bit dated. But then everything to do with that artificial, push-button lifestyle looks dated in the eighties. Ten years ago the London Bedding Centre, the only place in England where you can buy sheets of virtually any size, were making beds just like Hef's with stereos under the pillows and massage-amatics in the mattresses. These days there just is not the call for them any more, and a most popular bed is a copy of the Great Bed of Ware. It is nothing like the original of course and has no ghost to rattle the draperies but it does come seven feet square and with a canopy. Research has not revealed any copies of the celestial bed or indeed of the maharajah's silver bed but I am convinced it is the prohibitive cost that puts off the adventurous, and not lack of imagination. After all, in 1770, Chippendale's bill for state beds for Harewood House came to £6,326, which was a tidy sum in the eighteenth century. On examination of some of his more grandiose designs it is easy to see where the money went. His design for a state bed in 1761 recommends that: 'If the pedestals of the bedstead, the pillars, cornice and top of the dome are gilt burnished gold and the furniture is suitable the whole will look extremely grand. The bedstead should be 6 to 7 feet broad, 7 or 8 feet long and the whole height 14 or 15 feet. A workman of genius will easily comprehend the design.'

Sheraton's state beds were equally lavish but in a more refined way. He notes on one of his designs executed in 1803 for an English State Bed: 'The cornice, pillars, etc. are adorned with various symbolical figures expressive of the different branches of the British Government . . . Democracy, Aristocracy and Monarchy . . .'

Magnificent as such beds sound, they do not exercise the fascination of the Great Bed of Ware, the celestial bed and others mentioned above, because they are lifeless. It is the part beds play in the lives of their owners that makes them endlessly fascinating. A double bed is a place of fantasy, and one of deep delight. Only those who, as Shakespeare described in *Much Ado About Nothing*, 'know the heat of a luxurious bed' also know the guilty enjoyment to be had between its sheets. A double bed can ruin lives, create others and change the course of history. A double bed can also be the last sanctuary, a cosy refuge, a soft, enfolding friend to snuggle into and forget the ways of the world. As the poet John Donne observed, 'This bed thy centre is, these walls thy sphere.' ('The Sunne Rising')

In bed we laugh, in bed we cry
And born in bed, in bed we die.
The near approach a bed may show
Of human bliss to human woe.

BENSERADE, TR. DR JOHNSON

Double Beds for First-Timers

'Mama says you are to do what you like.'

THE CONTENTS OF A NOTE PINNED TO THE PILLOW OF A
YOUNG VICTORIAN BRIDE WHO HAD CHLOROFORMED
HERSELF FOR THE NIGHT RATHER THAN FACE A FATE
WORSE THAN DEATH, QUOTED BY SIR RICHARD BURTON IN
THE CUSTOMS AND MANNERS OF THE EAST

ONCE UPON A time first-timers were automatically virgins — or pretended they were. They approached their marriage beds with the utmost caution and not a little suspicion. After all, the only double bed most of them had ever seen at close quarters was the one in which they were conceived. These days, when adolescent sexual experience is as commonplace as teenage acne, it is a very brave man or woman who admits that a double bed, exposing itself in a large expanse of folded-back sheeting, is a daunting sight. How much easier it was in the old days to pretend innocence! Pretending experience is a much more demanding art. Of course it should not be necessary. The idea behind the permissive society was not only to admit honestly to sexual hopes, needs and desires, but to admit equally honestly when you did not have any. Unfortunately it has not turned out that way and the picture of the twentieth-century failure, at least for those interested in self-portraiture, is the overweight celibate with a lost libido. It is time to redress the balance. First-timers do exist just as they did in the distant past. They are still with us, clutching on to their dreams of wedded bliss and their life savings, and to them *The Double Bed Book* can offer concrete (or perhaps inner-sprung) advice.

There is, of course, the first-timer who is just as traditional if not quite as respectable. History tells of many young male virgins who were initiated in the art of love and its diversions by 'the older woman', often a professional older woman, outside marriage. Fathers considered it part of their parental duty to take a recently pubescent son by the hand and lead him to a familiar boudoir to learn a little about women and, in the

charming phrase of the time, 'to sow his wild oats'. Today such behaviour is giggled over in dinner-party conversation but the truth is that the role of the older woman in a young man's education has not changed drastically in the twentieth century, and some of the best pillow talk around begins with 'she taught me everything I know, darling'.

Then there are the first-timers who have not actually tied the knot but have been limiting their rehearsals to skirmishes on an inadequate single bed. Naturally the rules differ for each type of first-timer, as do the circumstances, and so in order to make everything crystal clear I shall divide the various first-timers into categories:

1) First sex, first marriage, first double bed   3 stars ★★★

2) First sex, first double bed   2 stars ★★

3) First double bed   1 star ★

THREE STARS ★★★

Congratulations! No matter what you have read elsewhere you are to be envied. You alone can enjoy the exquisite pain of doubt, fear, anticipation, excitement and fulfilment all at the same time. One of the sad truths of innocence and inexperience is that you do not appreciate them till they have gone, so it is much better to release them not only at the same time but with one you can honestly say you love nearly as much as you love yourself.

Three-starrers are inclined to think that they are an endangered species soon to be extinct. But there are more around than are prepared to own up. It is time they realized that the three-star category is one of maturity, perception and patience so that they too will come out of their closets and cry: 'I am a virgin. Where are my three stars?'

Top of the league of three-star first-timers is undoubtedly HRH the Princess of Wales. As the shy and vulnerable Lady Diana Spencer she had the world's press scarcely able to believe its ears when she protested she had no past. During Prince Charles's entire courtship of his lady, journalists around the world dug deep to find even a shred of evidence that could relegate her in the first-timer division but they had to emerge with their hands clean. Not a speck of dirt was to be found, which speaks volumes as the ladies and gentlemen of the press are unequalled as dirt-shovellers when they really put their minds to it. Single-handed 'Princess Diana' made virginity fashionable again, and as she walked down the aisle all in creamy white the entire British nation breathed a deep sigh of satisfaction. According to any religious or pagan rites *their* princess was properly dressed for the occasion. We do not know whether she keeps a diary, and not even the most gushing of court reporters can claim to know her feelings on her wedding night, but her great-great-great-grandmother-in-law, Queen Victoria, wrote frankly of her feelings after marriage to her perfect Albert. As a document to the joy and furious happiness of an innocent young girl the journal is unsurpassed.

10 FEBRUARY 1840
I never never spent such an evening! My dearest, dearest dear Albert sat on a footstool by my side and his excessive love and affection gave me feelings of heavenly love and happiness I never could have hoped to have felt before! He clasped me in his arms and we kissed each other again and again! His beauty sweetness and gentleness – really how can I ever be thankful enough to have such a husband! . . . to be called names of tenderness I have never yet heard used to me before was bliss beyond belief! Oh! this was the happiest day of my life! – May God help me to do my duty as I ought and be worthy of such blessings.

That physical pain of desire – all-consuming, all-devouring – is part of the terrifying gift of first-time love. Ibn H'azm, one of the first Andalucian poets of the tenth century, wrote of a young slave:

We understood each other. It was I who had her virginity and we loved each other deeply. Destiny took her from me . . . when she died I was not yet twenty and she was even younger . . . If ransom were possible I would buy her back with all my fortune. I would sacrifice a member of my body. I have never tasted real happiness since she died; I have never forgotten her. I have never been satisfied in the intimacy of other women. My love for her obliterated all my previous loves and rendered all that followed sacrilegious.

While in the simplistic but potent language of pop music in the 1980s the Stylistics sing: 'You, you make me feel brand new . . .' (Bell and Creed).

There are bound to be some three-starrers who find themselves at their moment of truth with one-starrers or even a no-starrer. Despite reams of evidence to the contrary this can make a three-starrer feel lost and at a distinct disadvantage, which is a pity. Sex is not a sport with love as a nil score. It is not meant to be treated as another performance to be later graded and marked from one to ten. To be a trembling innocent, willing but not terribly able to take on a double bed, is wildly attractive to even the most sophisticated and jaded double-bed user and some of the most cynical find after such an experience they feel just like three-starrers themselves – all over again.

For a pair of three-starrers who are confident of each other's total innocence, there are important considerations to be ironed out first, not the least of which is the choice of double bed. It is no good just going into the first department store on the high street and picking out one that looks the least embarrassing. This double bed of yours is going to share your lives. That it must be well sprung is obvious. That it must be solid is vital: comedians have been squeezing cheap laughs out of three-star first-timers since the first stand-up comic got to his feet. We laugh, as thousands before have laughed, because we're so grateful it's not happening to us. Someone else, not us, is the butt of the joke.

It is the essence of good comedy. Tragedy must always lurk beneath the surface for the laugh to work, and although a protesting double bed or, worse, one that collapses completely, may not seem to be tragic in theory, it is when it happens to you on your first night with the lover of your dreams. The way to avoid such catastrophes is to apply the time-honoured series of double-bed suitability tests:

DOUBLE-BED SUITABILITY TESTS

1) BOUNCABILITY

This is to be checked while the bed is still in the showroom; not to excess, you understand, but a bit of mild bouncing up and down is quite usual and should not cause other shoppers to stare.

2) SIZE

The ideal bed should not be too large: five feet wide is ideal. Although vast double beds are good for a nudge and a wink, they can look a bit like an over-dressed wrestling ring to a nervous three-starrer, and they are slightly obscene. Later on when that same three-starrer has acquired a certain confidence he/she could demand a huge bed, even a custom-made one, to accommodate the whole family including the dog, but that is for halcyon days ahead.

3) CREAKS

Your bed must not creak. Ideally creak-potential should be checked in the showroom but this is not easy, since tests, of necessity, attract attention. However, for those game enough to try, here they are: roll slowly from one side of the bed to the other in a continuous movement; repeat in the other direction; sit down on the bed suddenly together, and then try a discreet roll from side to side ending up in the middle; leap up from the bed. If none of these movements brings forth a single creak you are safe. You will also have attracted an interested audience.

However, when you have completed each of these tests satisfactorily you have found your bed. You have also revealed a confidence and determination any three-star companion would admire. Your future double-bed life bodes well. Good luck.

It is worth noting that three-starrers are not alone in their search for the ideal, solid, unassailable double bed. When Elizabeth Taylor was filming *Zee and Co.* in 1971 she insisted that she have a bed twice as deep as normal for a specially athletic scene in which she had to swing down from the chandelier on to the bed. Heals of London, bedmakers to the Queen (who are to beds what Rolls-Royce are to cars), were called upon to make one eighteen inches deep especially for Miss Taylor so that any crash landings would be suitably softened: all to no avail, as it turned out; the scene was cut. Another one-time three-starrer who understood the importance of the double bed was Jackie Onassis. When she was Mrs John Kennedy and first lady of the United States of America, she was so impressed with the British beds at the home of her sister, Princess Lee Radziwill, that she immediately ordered seven to be shipped back to the White House. It it said that life at the top is no bed of roses but Mrs Kennedy obviously put her trust in inner springs.

TWO STARS ★★

This is a popular category and a fascinating one in that the scales of experience must be unevenly balanced in one partner's favour. There can rarely be an example of two people enjoying first sex, first double bed at the same time, because someone had to buy the double bed in the first place and unless it is an investment for a special occasion, like a wedding night, most of us make do with what is available. If it is someone else's double bed then that someone is bound to be more knowing and adroit and therefore not a two-starrer. The popular idea of this kind of coupling is that of the older, mature man and the innocent, wide-eyed girl. Certainly this is one of life's great themes, widely embraced, like the lovers themselves, across the hemispheres. What is not quite as heavily advertised but every bit as popular is when the boot is on the other foot, so to speak, and the mature, experienced one is the woman of the piece.

Even in today's liberated times there is still considered something unvirile and shameful about a man who is a virgin. If women find themselves feeling alone and comparable to the dodo if they have managed to hang on to their virginity, how must men feel who are assumed to have been born with sexual expertise as part of their equipment, like ears?

The fearful anxiety and worry that accompanies a lack of practical knowledge in the sex department is almost too stressful to bear and male virgins of fifteen are known to pore over every available magazine or earnest 'how to do it' booklet despairing that it looks and seems more and more complicated by the minute. Then comes salvation: the older woman. Unlike the girls of his own generation the older woman in a young man's life revels in his inexperience. You can't teach an old dog new tricks, she reckons, but with care you can groom a puppy into a real thoroughbred. An older woman has patience, she has tolerance and she has appreciation. In her deep double bed far away from the hurly burly of the long chase, let alone the chaise longue, a young man's fantasy can turn into glowing reality in the space of an afternoon.

One of the most famous older-woman/younger-man liaisons was that between the writer George Eliot and her young lover, John Cross. George Eliot (1819–80), born Mary Ann Evans and twenty-one years older than Mr Cross, was quite breathtakingly ugly and notably lacking in traditional feminine charms but she was blessed with an inescapable attraction and he idolized her. She finally agreed to marry him when she was sixty-one, just eight months before she died. He was forty years old. But the experience cannot have been all joy for him: he jumped into a canal during their Venetian honeymoon.

George Sand (1804–76), who shared more with Ms Eliot than a mere pseudonym, fell deeply in love with Poland's favourite son, the composer Frederic Chopin, and although she was only six years older than he was, she nursed the belief that thousands of older women have had before and since. She convinced herself she was a mother figure to him.

APRIL 1834
Whether I have been mistress or mother to you what does that matter? Whether I have inspired you by love or by friendship, whether I have been happy or unhappy with you, nothing of this affects the present state of my mind. I know that I love you, that is all . . .

Oh my child, my child! How much I need your tenderness and your forgiveness . . .

To find the attraction an older woman holds for a younger man is to search for the indefinable. There is no such thing as an 'it' you can put your finger on. As with style, you can tell who has it but you cannot spell out what it is.

Some people have it and make it pay
Some people can't even give it away . . .
'GYPSY' STEIN/SONDHEIM

Sarah Bernhardt (1845–1923) had 'it' in spades. The divine Sarah who was known in her prime as the eighth wonder of the world had 'it' even in her declining years, inspiring a fledgling writer, Pierre Loüys, to enter in his diary after seeing her at the age of forty-three:

Oh! Sarah! Sarah! Sarah is grace! Sarah is youth! Sarah is beauty! Sarah is divinity! I am mad, I am beside myself! I no longer know what I am doing. I no longer think of anything. I saw Sarah Bernhardt last night. My God! What a woman! Sarah . . . Sarah . . . when shall I see you again? I weep, I tremble, I grow mad. Sarah I love you!

Such youthful enthusiasm must have been extremely gratifying for the wonderful, if middle-aged Sarah. I prefer the more laconic but no less devoted response that the late one-time sex symbol Diana Dors received from her young actor husband, Alan Lake. When Miss Dors was comfortably nudging fifty and 200 lb, she enquired, 'Darling, will you love me when I'm old and fat?'

'Yes and I do,' he answered.

Unfortunately not all older-woman/younger-man liaisons signal the beginning of a long-standing affair. Older women who take on two-starrers do so at their peril because once versed in the arts of love erstwhile two-starrers cannot wait to find other two-starrers to impress with their technique. A two-starrer is delightful and he will remember his teacher with love and gratitude but when he confides that he is investing in a double bed all of his own it is the beginning of the end of the affair.

It is all quite different when the wily teacher with the ultimate in double beds is male. Once his shy little two-starrer has decided on a course of blissful submission, she too will be a willing and apt pupil. Her enthusiasm will astound him and she could end up making an old man not only very happy but somewhat breathless. However, unlike her male counterpart who can't wait to get out there and let others in on his bedroom secrets, she will probably mistake the delight she feels in her new-found sexuality for love. Most women fall in love with the man who deflowered them and when the seduction is performed with tact and gentleness, her vulnerable heart has no chance. Some men, particularly the older ones, are mindful of this responsibility and if there is any letting down it is done with a certain amount of sensitivity. But not all seducers are gentlemen and it must be pointed out that there are a great many some-time two-starrers walking about nursing bruised egos and broken hearts. The pity of it is that there is no set of rules to follow or tests to apply that will separate the gentlemen from the swine. Most play the honesty game these days. Most of them murmur, with a rakish smile, that they are not promising anything but by God the two of you could be unbelievable together. Most of them will later insist, some kindly, some like small boys who have tired of a favourite toy, that nothing is for keeps any more and how boring it would be if it was. So the tearful two-starrer has not got a leg to stand on — or often — a bed to sleep in.

What she must never do, however, not even in her darkest moments, is to deny that love existed in the first place.

> *After all, my erstwhile dear,*
> *My no longer cherished*
> *Need we say it was not love,*
> *Now that love has perished.*
> EDNA ST VINCENT MILLAY

or, to put it another way . . . 'Time wounds all heels.' (JANE ACE).

ONE STAR ★

This undoubtedly constitutes the most popular category. If all its members were laid end to end, as Dorothy Parker would say, nobody would be at all surprised. One-starrers come in all shapes and sizes and in all three sexes. The age group rarely extends beyond the early thirties and they are usually fairly cheerful types who treat their first double bed with a certain respect and gratitude. After all, they know what it is like in a single. One-starrers are known for their inventiveness and athleticism, gleaned, no doubt, from experiences on their parents' sofa, in the linen cupboard and the back seat of an ancient Ford. They are often inconsiderate sleepers and can be found stretched diagonally across the bed in what may seem to be a selfish fashion. Experienced double-bed users should realize that it is not that they are being thoughtless, they just cannot believe they have got all this space.

One-starrers are quick learners, and it is quite usual to find them sneaking out before it seems proper, on the pretext that they have urgent business requiring immediate attention. Do not be fooled. The urgent business is quite often at the nearest bed shop. Once initiated into double-bed life one-starrers cannot wait to become full-time double-bed users themselves. Oh well — bed riddance!

A Diversion
The Hollywood Treatment

Reel 1

THE MOVIE .... MALE AND FEMALE
THE STAR .... GLORIA SWANSON
THE DIRECTOR .... CECIL B. DE MILLE
THE YEAR 1919

THE CAMERA PEEKS through the keyhole into milady's bedroom. It is intimate, it is sensuous and it is glamorous. This is a lady whose lingerie is French, whose bedspread is silk, whose lifestyle is lavish. Oh sigh! Oh Gloria! And the next day another thousand American housewives nag their husbands for a double bed with a gilded headboard – like Gloria's – and a bedspread of some sort of satiny stuff – like Gloria's. Is it any wonder

Awkward perhaps – but feet still firmly anchored: Greta Garbo and John Barrymore, <u>Grand Hotel</u>, 1932. KOBAL COLLECTION

that during the post-war prosperity of America in the 1920s the sales of double beds took seventy-five per cent of the available market? Gloria Swanson, Pola Negri and Greta Garbo were among the glittering figures of the silver screen, and in the hands of showmen like Cecil B. de Mille and the lesser-known director Clarence Brown they pranced around their silken boudoirs as to the bedside-manner born. They received considerable instruction in this department from the truly expert Elinor Glyn. She was a lady of many parts, who always had her eye on the main chance. At the very height of her notoriety as a writer of daring novels she took herself off to Hollywood and became counsellor of love to the stars. Her best-known pupils were Gloria Swanson, the 'It' girl, Clara Bow, and Rudolph Valentino.

These were the heady, light-hearted days of Hollywood movie-making and they could not last. Even the great Cecil B. de Mille realized that the puritans would need appeasing and introduced one scene in *Male and Female* with the legend 'Why shouldn't the bedroom express as much art as the drawing-room?' written up on the screen as a not very subtle sub-title. He did not fool anyone. The good respectable folk of Hollywood, and in the 1920s there were still one or two, were already getting extremely hot and bothered by what was coming up on the movie screens and were in the process of defining a code of moral standards that the motion-picture industry would have to abide by. By 1930 they had found it and by 1934 it had happened: the dreaded Production Code was enforced by the even more dreaded Hays Office.

A great many workers in the Hollywood dream factory believed that it was Mae West and lines such as: 'Is that a gun you're wearing or are you just pleased to see me?' that provided the red rag to the Hays Office bull but it was Garbo, the epitome, you would think, of screen artistry and perfection who really incensed them. She had a kind of despairing, passionate sex appeal that burst on the screen.

'John Gilbert sweeps Garbo off her feet!' screamed the fan magazines. And so he did, straight into bed. Their scenes together, particularly in *The Flesh and the Devil* (1927) were like 'a tumultuous volcano'.

Unfortunately what erupted out of this volcano was a furious determination by the outraged moralists that this just would not do. *Queen Christina*, where she revealed the sexuality that existed between her and her lover by caressing everything as she moved around their bedroom, giving the objects and lifeless furniture a sexuality of their own, was damned as blatant wickedness. But the final crunch came with a little-known film starring Miriam Hopkins, *The Story of Temple Drake*. It was based on William Faulkner's novel, *Sanctuary*, and therefore considered by everyone except the Hays Office to be an artistic enterprise. The fact that the star, Miss Hopkins, played an unmarried gangster's moll who went to bed with her lover was bad enough; that she enjoyed it was the last straw. After *The Story of Temple Drake* nothing was safe. Men and women, married or not, were not to be depicted in bed together. The way film directors got around this ruling was to make out the stars were not *really* in bed together if one of the lovers had a foot on the floor. Hence we see Norma Shearer's extremely modest and over-dressed Juliet with her Romeo anchored to the floor as if his life depended on it. And so it did in

Gloria Swanson, back where she belongs, on a double bed in <u>Sunset Boulevard,</u> 1950: RONALD GRANT COLLECTION

movie terms. No foot, no Romeo, no film. It was the cause of much hilarity in the far naughtier world of theatrical revue when musical numbers like this appeared in the early 1940s:

We're keeping one foot on the floor m'dears,
We're keeping one foot on the floor
We know that it's senseless
'But the censor's incensed us
We're keeping one foot on the floor.

When a love scene's potentially torrid
And the censor is perfectly horrid
With one foot on the floor
We then know what's in store
Not much more than a kiss on the forehead

Reel 3

The only producer to beat the system while it held sway was the redoubtable Howard Hughes. His movie *The Outlaw* made in 1943 and starring Jane Russell and her bosom featured a scene in which Miss Russell climbed into bed with her co-star Jack Beutel. She just had to. Otherwise, according to the script, the poor man would have died of cold. For three years Hughes battled over this scene with the Hays Office and the Legion of Decency, with Hughes refusing to give way. The film was finally released in 1946 with both this scene and the vital Motion Picture Association Certificate, which was the industry's seal of approval. Howard Hughes had won. The movie was a huge success, but lesser producers found the price of independence too high. Twin beds became the law in Hollywood and by the 1950s sales of double beds had plummeted from a comfortable seventy-five per cent of the market in the 1920s to only thirty-two per cent. It was cause of much concern; so much so in fact that no less a man than the director of the Family Relations Institute protested in the press: 'This movement towards twin beds must stop. It was started by furniture dealers who make twice as much money selling two beds instead of one. Besides the change from a double bed to twin beds is often the prelude to divorce.'

Of course it was not really the fault of avaricious furniture dealers at all. They were simply cashing in on a trend. It was Myrna Loy and William Powell who started it. Sleeping as they did in twin singles as the devastating Nick and Nora Charles in the *Thin Man* series, while being madly sophisticated about everything else, gave double beds a bad name. Suddenly the friendly, sexy double bed had a kind of incestuous look about it, and American housewives went out in droves in search of the smart new singles. Once the rot had set in with Myrna and Bill there was no stopping the change to single beds. (The magic formula of a loving couple of smart private detectives immortalized in the *Thin Man* series in the 1930s lives on these days in *Hart to Hart*, the television series starring Robert Wagner and Stephanie Powers. They too are beautiful, rich and supposedly dead

The world's most sophisticated couple, Nick and Nora, were instrumental in tearing the American double bed asunder: Myrna Loy and William Powell in Dashiell Hammett's Song of the Thin Man, 1936. NATIONAL FILM ARCHIVE, LONDON

Jayne Mansfield always did try hard – either with a partner...
KOBAL COLLECTION

...or without! Promises! Promises! 1963. KOBAL COLLECTION

chic. The difference is that where Bill Powell as Nick Charles used to smoke like a chimney and get rip-roaring drunk in low bars Jonathan Hart has never let the filthy weed near his lips and when he orders a drink from the bar it is a club soda with a twist of lemon. In the bedroom, however, Jennifer and Jonathan snuggle down together and do not give a damn about where their feet end up. How values change!)

The actress who really built her career on the innocent naughtiness of a pair of singles was Doris Day. Films with titles like *Pillow Talk* turned out to be about pillow talk between beds with a wall in the middle. It was all very pert and wide-eyed and wedding-ring-on-the-finger-in-the-last-reel. Meanwhile, as social commentators continued to drone on about art imitating life, there was solid proof that life, in fact, imitated art as bedrooms up and down the nation were split by single beds. Then came the revolution!

Reel 4

In 1953 Otto Preminger made *The Moon is Blue* starring Maggie Macnamara and William Holden and included in the film were three vital factors — two lines of dialogue and one bit of direction:

> *Girl to man: 'Are you going to seduce me?'*
> *Girl to man: 'I'm a virgin you know.'*
> *Man and girl are seen to go upstairs to a bedroom fully intent on making love.*

The Hays Office and the Catholic Legion of Decency had a joint fit but it made no difference. *The Moon is Blue* was released without the hitherto vital Motion Picture Association Certificate and although it was not accepted in certain cinemas, it was still an overriding, unqualified success. There was a total collapse of the influence of the ogres who had been riding Hollywood for the past twenty years. Six years later two British films performed the death rites on the Hays Office and its power. In 1959 *Look Back in Anger* featured a bed that was not merely a double but an unmade double with its skirts about its knees. The movie-going public barely had a moment to suck in its breath and wait for the sky to fall in

Marlon Brando, whose lovemaking in the movies has rarely been in anything
quite as traditional as a double bed, breaks the mould with Rita Moreno in
Night of the Following Day, 1969: RONALD GRANT COLLECTION

before *Room at the Top* was released the same year with a sympathetic
treatment of an adulterous affair between the hero Joe Lambton, played by
Laurence Harvey, and his French mistress, the glorious Simone Signoret.

So after twenty years of enforced retirement the double bed began to
make its comeback, triumphantly celebrated with *Cat on a Hot Tin Roof*
starring two of Hollywood's most solid box-office draws, Paul Newman and
Elizabeth Taylor. 'Cat' did not stop at *featuring* a double bed, it was *about*
a double bed and actually included the line spoken by Big Momma played
by Judith Anderson: 'When a marriage goes on the rocks the rocks are
there,' thumping the bed soundly, 'right *there*.'

'Reel 5'

Today, rocks or not, double beds are back in the movies. They are the big
stars, and the more abandoned, decadent and outrageous they look the

better. Producers who spy old-fashioned brass models in the dusty recesses of out-of-town antique shops get quite carried away and offer ridiculous sums of money. 'I can make you a star,' they whisper, and off goes another double bed seduced by the vision of fame, fortune and a creakingly good time somewhere over the rainbow.

Unfortunately we who know Hollywood have seen it before. The stars start believing their own publicity and think they do not need anyone any more. One young bed ended up in *Barbarella* with Jane Fonda, and became not just a sexual arena but a seducer to boot. Never before or since has a bed actually *done the seducing*. Of course *Barbarella* was filmed in the sixties and it all happened long before Jane Fonda found herself or her politics or the Californian Stretch, and will never happen again. But many a young hopeful double bed with a soul has wound up disillusioned with the Hollywood mirage of stardom. The pity is that romance is dead in the movies. Bring back Gloria Swanson and her temples of love. Elinor Glyn, where are you now that we need you?

The Art of Keeping a Mistress

Isn't she lovely, 'the mistress'?
With her wide-apart grey-green eyes,
The droop of her lips and, when she smiles,
Her glance of amused surprise?

How nonchalantly she wears her clothes,
How expensive they are as well
And the sound of her voice is as soft and deep
As the Christ Church tenor bell.

But why do I call her 'the mistress'
Who know not her way of life?
Because she has more of a cared-for air
Than many a legal wife . . .

FROM 'LENTEN THOUGHTS OF A HIGH ANGLICAN', JOHN
BETJEMAN

I MET MY first mistress and my first unmarried double bed on the same afternoon. I had been taken, aged seventeen, to see my great-aunt, Beth, who was famous in our family for being a bit wild. She had run away when she was nineteen to be a Ziegfeld Follies girl and although she did not actually make it she did meet a hugely wealthy financier who wore white suits with a red carnation in his buttonhole and she was his mistress for over thirty years. When I got around to meeting Auntie Beth she was nearly seventy and had given up active service, so to speak, quite a few years earlier, but her wealthy lover still cared for her and provided for her and kept her in a deliciously pretty flat overlooking the harbour in Sydney, Australia. She called it 'my little den of iniquity' and insisted, despite my other more conventional aunt's protestations, on showing me all around. And there it was: the bed.

I now understand why the middle-class English of Victorian times covered the legs of their pianos to protect the innocent. Auntie Beth's bed had the most provocative legs. Bold and brass they were, peeping from underneath their lace petticoats in a most unseemly way and the expanse of bed they supported was embarrassingly large. Auntie Beth obviously took her mistressly role very seriously and knew what was expected of her. The coverlet was of oyster satin, the underskirts were lace, and all over the bed were lots and lots of cushions made of silks and satins, embroidered with thoughts like 'home is where the heart is' and 'love is like a red, red rose'.

Auntie Beth died easily and comfortably in her sleep a good twenty years ago aged eighty. She never married, never dallied with any man except her favourite lover and never lost her sense of fun. I was a very young and naïve seventeen when I met her but she managed to make me feel as if I too had the makings of a mistress when she insisted that she inspect my waist (quite good), my ankles (less good), and kindly pronounced me fitted with the right equipment for her calling, if not the inclination. Alas, even then in the frustrated fifties, before the rise of the permissive society, mistresses were beginning to feel the chill wind of change blowing up their skirts. I had a sneaking suspicion that even if I'd dared follow in my great-aunt's footsteps my career would have been depressingly short. She probably didn't realize it at the time but she was one of the last of a dying breed. In her day mistresses were wicked and exotic and the fact that they supplied sexual favours to men who were not their husbands placed them beyond the pale and made them dangerous to know. These days they've been taken over by enthusiastic amateurs. Everyone's at it but somehow the style and the discreet charm have gone, trampled underfoot in the rush to show how liberated we all are. How can a mistress thrive in a climate that condones and actively encourages that which used to be branded 'original sin'?

In a society where marriage is becoming déclassé in smart circles and where virgin brides belong only to history books the mistress has a tough time maintaining her status, not to mention her flat, her car and her account at Yves Saint Laurent.

· Of course there are still those who call themselves mistresses but they are not what they were. A mistress's byword was her discretion. Even the most famous of the famous mistresses of kings and emperors, who had position and power and quite often ended up with a title, would never be so gross as to mention to her lover's wife that she, the mistress, was the true object of his affections. There were better ways of displaying power and status than through mere word of mouth, for example when two of Louis

XIV of France's mistresses passed each other on the Queen's Staircase at Versailles. Quoth up-and-coming mistress, the Marquise de Maintenon to her earlier rival, the Marquise de Montespan: 'You are going down, madam? I am going up.'

Mistresses in living memory, like my dear departed Auntie Beth, would have died rather than call up their protectors at the family home. It just was not done and was considered a sign of ill-breeding to stoop to such a level. There were six commandments a mistress had to abide by, and they were unbreakable and unquestioned.

THE MISTRESS'S CHARTER

1) Thou shalt not be jealous.
2) Thou shalt not expect to see thy lover at weekends, birthdays, anniversaries, school speech days and during the whole of August when he takes the family abroad.
3) Thou shalt respect his wife at all times and never refer to her as 'her', 'the bitch' or 'your little woman at home'.
4) Thou shalt be faithful to thy lover even though thou knowest that the same cannot be said for him.
5) Thou shalt accept every small gift with delighted squeals of appreciation and thou shalt not gnash thy teeth at the correspondingly larger gift that will be considered 'her' due.
6) In the unlikely event that thou shouldst ever be confronted by his wife and accused of being his mistress thou shalt deny everything and continue so to do until hell freezes over.

In return for the slavish adherence to these six simple commandments a mistress could expect to be kept, to have to think of little except whether she should wear the satin lounging pyjamas or the bare essentials, and to keep the sheets clean and the champagne chilled. It has to be admitted that it was not a bad life for the fortunate few whose protectors stayed with them after their smiles had faded and their bosoms dropped; and as Eartha Kitt once remarked, 'It's a hell of a lot better than pickin' cotton.' Sadly women who are good mistress material today just do not look upon it in the same light. The very suggestion that they should be *kept* is anathema. Have some man pay for her flat, her clothes, her car? How loathsome, how degrading, how vile! She thinks it is much better to squeeze into the rush-hour in the morning, to type or file or talk on the telephone all day, only to squeeze on to the underground again in the evening and get paid a dishonest wage for an honest day's work. Of course, if she then goes out to dinner, goes back to his place and behaves just like a mistress but in his bachelor single instead of her unmarried double and with nothing to look forward to except a couple of hours' sleep before she gets up again, that is her business. The enterprising woman who does opt for a mistress's lot is of another breed altogether.

Basically there are two types: the first is a kind of dream creature who was brought up on novels about Madame Pompadour and Nell Gwyn. She harbours all sorts of romantic notions about the influence a good mistress can have over her lover, and believes sincerely in the adage 'behind every successful man there's a good woman'. As his wife cannot possibly be a good woman ('otherwise why is he with *me*?') she thinks that must mean her. She is a remarkably generous girl who is only a mistress after a fashion as she pays for her own flat, food and clothes, and squeaks with pleasure at the odd fiver he throws her way for the concoction of the romantic little dinners *à deux*. Her specialities are fragrant things cooked lovingly in wine and followed by some light *soupçon* of nothing, designed to sit gently on the stomach so as not to interrupt his sexual fervour. Unfortunately, unless she's a French mistress and highly organized (more of this later), the one time she has cooked dinner for him is the one time he has hurried round to see her after rushing his way through a huge family meal at home, and any sexual fervour that is left after two dinners in the space of an hour is strictly in the imagination. But this is just another stitch in life's rich tapestry for the ideal first type of mistress.

'We have to take the rough with the smooth,' she murmurs tenderly stroking his five o'clock shadow that won't be removed until he gets home in case 'she' gets suspicious. Other similar little stitches such a mistress has to cope with are little-known facts of life such as, just when she has chosen the lounging pyjamas, the champagne is chilled and the sheets are crispy clean her mother's best friend rings to say mother is having one of her turns and could she come over at once. Or her own best friend rings up tearful and in need of at least an hour's consolation over a lost job, man or opportunity. There have been many contributory factors in the gradual death of the old-fashioned mistress and although the permissive society and the women's movement between them have a great deal to answer for, twentieth-century living can take part of the blame too. Mistresses do not live in ivory towers any more. And even if they did who could afford them?

The second type of mistress is, regrettably, a far commoner species. For her there are no rules and nothing is sacrosanct; witness the most scandalous 'mistress' story of the decade that broke in 1983. The famous 'Parkinson Sex Case' when the thirty-year-old Sarah Keays was revealed to be the mistress of Cecil Parkinson, Chairman of the British Conservative Party. Ms Keays not only broke all the rules, she rewrote the mistress's code when she published her side of the story in *The Times*. Today's so-called mistress will not only kiss and tell, she will kiss and tell: the world's press, her lawyers, and his wife. One story that circulated post-Parkinson went like this:

*First politician: 'I never slept with my wife before we were married —
did you?'*
Second politician: 'I don't know. What was her maiden name?'

As British families relished each new development in the Parkinson case, on the other side of the Atlantic American households had just recovered from their most fascinating sex scandal, when twenty-seven-year-old Vicki Morgan, one-time mistress of the department store millionaire, sixty-six-year-old Alfred Bloomingdale, had gone to court accusing her lover's wife of jealousy.

The old-fashioned mistress may be aghast at such happenings, but the truth is that she looks decidedly *passée* as she attempts to gift-wrap her charms in soft lights, sweet music and Chanel No.5. Such refinements have no place in our tough little world of equal opportunities and his'n'her dungarees. And is it not a pity? Mistresses may have been a product of corrupt times, but they were enormous fun.

Elinor Glyn, who was more famous in 1907 as the writer of a passionate little novella called *Three Weeks* than for her mistressly powers over Lord Curzon, inspired the lines:

> *Would you rather sin with Elinor Glyn*
> *On a tiger skin*
> *Or would you prefer*
> *To err with her*
> *On some other fur?*

It is said that Curzon himself supplied Miss Glyn with her tiger skin, but she certainly never restricted herself to it. She was also known to strew her bed with rose petals, no doubt under the impression that presentation is all-important – a sort of Constance Spry of her time perhaps. English matrons who could only contemplate dipping into her novel armed with a plentiful supply of smelling salts were outraged as they read Elinor Glyn's explicit passages. Where did she ever learn such things? Literally at the feet of one of the truly great British mistresses, Lillie Langtry.

Once while preparing herself for a visit by her most famous lover, King Edward VII, Mrs Langtry found two little girls hiding under the skirts of her dressing-table. The one taking notes was Elinor Glyn. Of course, the Jersey Lily did no end of good for the mistress's image. While obeying each of the six commandments to the letter, she was known, not only in the court, but throughout the country, as a profound and important influence on the king. When he died she received a stack of nicely laundered hankies that she had mislaid over the years in the royal apartments. The sender was the queen, who accompanied the return of Mrs Langtry's property with a note of condolence on their joint loss.

If the queen had set out to write letters of condolence to all her husband's mistresses, she would have developed writer's cramp. There were Hortense Schneider in Paris, French and English society flowers like the Princesse de Sagan, the Duchesse de Mouchy, Lady Brooke, Lady Warwick and Mrs Keppel. A lesser-known but wondrously extravagant delight of the king's bedchamber was a girl called Emma Crouch. It was not a name that tripped off the tongue easily so she changed it to Cora Pearl and carved a brilliant career for herself moving from one member of the European aristocracy to another. An actress, she was said to bathe in champagne and was rumoured to have earned and spent the phenomenal sum of £15,000,000 during her lavish reign.

A much earlier, but still enormously popular, British mistress was Nell Gwyn, who, as every schoolchild knows, used to sell oranges before she caught the eye and eventually the heart of King Charles II. She was everything a mistress should be: no ideas above her station, no false sense of grandeur, a product of those bawdy unselfconscious times. As an anonymous versifier of the seventeenth century put it:

Hard by 'Pall Mall lives a wench call'd Nell.
King Charles II doth keep her.
She hath got a trick to handle his prick
'But never lays hand on his sceptre.
All matters of state from her soul she does hate,
And leave to the politic bitches.
'The whore's in the right, for 'tis her delight
'To be scratching just where it itches.

She could not read or write, but she had a good honest streak of common sense that came to her aid in the most hair-raising situations. Once, in 1681, her carriage was held up by a particularly unpleasant mob under the impression that she was her rival, the French Catholic Louise de Kérouaille. 'Good people,' she cried, 'let me pass. I am the *Protestant* whore.'

She was always mindful of her place in the king's life and the most elaborate and expensive piece of furniture in her house at 79 Pall Mall was her solid silver bedstead, bought from one John Coques or Cognes, a silversmith whose shop was on the other side of Pall Mall. Much later, after her death, the bill for this extravagance was found. Nell's silver bedstead, with silver at two shillings and eleven pence an ounce, had cost over £900. It had been melted down to pay for 'pressing liabilities' facing Nellie after the king's death.

It is easy to have fun at Nell's expense as she was a cheerful, unassuming girl who would as soon join in the laughter as object to it, but she had her own dignity and when the king died she revealed the closeness of their relationship in a letter written on her behalf to the new king. It not only has a touching simplicity but sums up the perfect relationship between man and mistress: 'Had he lived he told me before he died that the world should see by what he did for me that he had both love and value for me. He was my friend and allowed me to tell him all my griefs and did like a friend advise me and told me who was my friend and who was not.'

According to the romantic novelist and authority on the British royal family Barbara Cartland, the monarchy owes a huge debt to Nell Gwyn and similar women of humble origins. 'The reason why the Bourbons and all the French lot got their heads cut off,' she says, 'is because they became too inbred, too apart from their people, whereas we British have always rather gone for the common touch. They brought in a bit of good red blood to mix with the blue which was terribly healthy, both physically and politically.' That Nell Gwyn contributed to the British aristocracy is a matter of history. Soon after she had given birth to her first child, a son, she was playing with him by the river at Salisbury Hall (just a few miles from the old Roman town of St Albans). She said to the king, 'If you don't give him a title I'll throw him in.'

'Put down the Duke of St Albans at once,' said Charles II, and there have been Dukes of St Albans ever since, all direct descendants of Charles and his Nellie.

Unfortunately not all English monarchs were such gentlemen. William IV, while he was still Duke of Clarence, dallied long enough with his mistress, a kindly lady called Mrs Jordan, to have five sons and five daughters by her. She too was an actress, but apparently not as content as Nell Gwyn. The very presence of the ten children and the need to provide for them made the forty-six-year-old duke start looking for an heiress who would marry him and provide him with the wherewithal to pay his debts. Although Mrs Jordan was allocated a reasonable pension, she was defrauded of her money. She died in poverty, heartbroken, having fled to France to outwit her creditors. Fourteen years later her sometime lover became King of England.

An unfortunate attitude towards their mistresses seems to have been a family failing. William's brother, the Duke of York, kept the charming and witty Mary Anne Clarke as his mistress until he dumped her for a fleeting affair with another actress, Mrs Carey. During her short reign, however, Mary Anne Clarke proved herself to be a British mistress in the true Nell Gwyn tradition. When the grand old Duke of York, who was not as jolly as the nursery rhyme suggests, refused to increase her allowance above a paltry one thousand pounds a year (pleading a severe and permanent cash flow problem) Mary Anne saw to matters herself. For a standard fee she would ensure that the names of army officers seeking promotion reached the duke, who was Commander in Chief of the army. She pinned each list of names to the curtains above her bed. In the morning when her contented royal lover had gone her list had gone with him. The resulting promotions appeared quite promptly in the London Gazette.

Although British mistresses have flown the flag with vigour and with enthusiasm there can be no mistresses, past or present, to rival the French. Even today as mistresses are replaced by live-in girlfriends in the rest of the Western world, the tradition in France of '*cinq à sept*' still lives. Five o'clock is the accepted time for a French husband to leave the office to dally with his mistress and still be home by seven with his wife and family. French men maintain that the reason that they have been able to keep the mistress habit alive is because they are so adorable and sexy and sophisticated. What they forget to mention is that France is a Catholic country where divorce is still frowned upon. In Britain and the United States the change of partners is given a surface respectability by the exchanges of marriage vows – over and over again – while in France men tend to stick to the same legal partner with a mistress on the side. In Britain such an arrangement is crudely known as 'a leg-over'. In France it is a '*jambe en l'air*' – naturally.

At first glance it would appear that little has changed since Gigi's day when the delicious heroine of Colette's novel was initiated by her ambitious aunt into the secrets of mistressdom. In fact it is all quite different. In those days a chap's wife was the last person to be given the glad eye. These days she is quite often the first, and amongst the Parisian bourgeoisie there is a coterie of wives who have taken up mistressing as a hobby – like rose growing or stamp collecting. As with most hobbies, being a mistress is terribly time-consuming and requires organizational ability *par excellence*. This is inclined to detract a little from the '*je ne sais quoi*' of

Greta Garbo – no doubt dressed for a different occasion: <u>Mata Hari</u>, 1932.
Kobal Collection

the affair but even though they feel something is not quite right French men do not like to complain.

'She's got it down to a fine art,' explained one gentleman apologetically. 'She prepares two cassoulets, two salades vertes and even ices two bottles of Montrachet. One dinner for two is for us, the other for her and her husband.' He did not like to nag but there were times as he lay there listening to the effects of the cassoulet rumbling about his stomach that he felt a ghastly presentiment. In a few hours 'he' would not only partake of the same delights, satisfy the same appetites but make the same noises afterwards. *Merde!* Coping with such relationships takes a great deal of 'savoir faire' or total lack of interest. The author Douglas Sutherland tells a story of the two French men:

> *First French man: 'I think you should know,* mon vieux, *I am sleeping with your wife.'*
> *Second French man: 'Oh really? Is she any good at it these days?'*

Such organization and indifference to the all-important double bed must have the great French mistresses of the past turning in their graves. Gabrielle d'Estrées, who was mistress of Henri IV of France, would be amazed. When she could not make up her mind which colour to have her bed, she had twelve made, all embellished with silver and gold and occasional extravagances such as coverlets sewn with pearls. She was obviously determined that the king should not be bored in her bed, even if he occasionally wondered where he was. Flushed with success, she soon decided that her first twelve beds should be used only in winter and commissioned another twelve for the summer months. What she did with the other twenty-three beds when they were not in use is not revealed, but as Gabrielle was a resourceful creature she must have thought of something.

Any French mistress worthy of the title was well aware that she had to gather rosebuds while she could and she made sure the season lasted as long as possible. It seems crude to term bedroom nick-nacks 'tools of the trade', but the great mistresses probably saw them in that light and surrounded themselves with the most luxurious accessories they could find. Their patronage of furniture-makers kept the industry alive and it is partly due to them that there was such variety and beauty in bedroom design during the reign of Louis XIV. In his excellent history of the bed, *Warm and Snug*, Lawrence Wright describes a visit to the court of the Sun King by the Siamese Ambassador. While on a tour around the Royal Bed Store His Excellency was shown at least sixty glorious beds; and there were over three hundred more, if only he had had the time to see them all.

The king's most intelligent and dazzling mistress, the witty Madame de Maintenon found her lover's own bedchamber too draughty for words. 'If I have to stay any longer in the king's chamber,' she wrote, 'I shall end up paralysed.' Naturally she remedied matters in her own room at Versailles. Her great bed had columns nine feet high topped by plumes, and green and gold hangings lined with red. She supplemented this with a small *lit de repos*, or daybed, to match.

There were literally hundreds of these brilliant and remarkable ladies who made their mark in a most satisfying way on the history of the Western world, but alas their day is over. The reason why the mistress habit developed as satisfyingly as it did was that there were hard and fast

A woman's chastity is a stye in the Devil's Eye! The Devil's Eye, 1960.
Jarl Kolle and Bibi Andersson: THE RONALD GRANT COLLECTION

social rules in the old days, not the least of which was 'Thou shalt marry a lady who will be a social and financial asset to the family'. Today, when people marry whom they please or even do not marry at all, the scope for mistress-keeping is becoming more and more limited. You cannot be the mistress of a man who is having a 'relationship'. It just does not work, and although there are men who may hanker after a mistress but not a wife, they cannot have one. A true mistress-keeper has to abide by the rules of the game, and the first rule is that you cannot commit adultery if you are not married.

In the absence of a comprehensive guide to the regulations of mistress-keeping the following should prove useful. It must be added, however, that mistress-keeping like bee-keeping has its hazards, chiefly the likelihood of being stung.

ON BEING A MISTRESS-KEEPER

1) A mistress-keeper should make a complete study of the species before the commencement of any nesting, i.e. the putting of a down-payment on an apartment.

2) A mistress-keeper must at all times display kindness towards the species and keep any evidence of temper, mood, tetchiness for home, where it is expected.

3) A mistress-keeper should strenuously avoid any evidence of his hobby, i.e. the production of children.

4) No mistress-keeper shall exhibit meanness or advanced thriftiness in necessities such as: the paying of the rent; the continuation of the charge account at a well-known store; occasional lunches at an out-of-town but modish restaurant.

5) Should a mistress-keeper eventually tire of his hobby he is obliged to allow his mistress to keep the apartment and, if one was supplied, the car. If this seems extreme it should be remembered that under modern law she is probably entitled to them.

A mere glance through this potted guide will reveal to most interested parties that mistress-keeping has its drawbacks, not the least of which is the expense. There was a time when it was possible to keep a mistress just out of town in relative luxury for a comparatively small investment. In London the favourite mistress colony was in Hamilton Terrace, St John's Wood. This address had a certain cachet in that it was named after one of England's most famous and exotic mistresses, Emma, Lady Hamilton, beloved of Admiral Nelson. In New York, city of several thriving mistress colonies, a favoured spot used to be Sutton Place. Today such an address would speak volumes for her protector, as he would have to be as rich as several Rockefellers and Sheik Yamani rolled into one to pay for it. These days areas like Queens and White Plains are within the realms of possibility. However, little bijou apartments, albeit on the outskirts of town, are not cheap. The frustrated lover may be able to cope with the rent, rates and maintenance, but the cost of petrol consumed travelling back and forth could kill his ardour.

The other truly maddening aspect of mistress-keeping is that it is not tax-deductible. Interestingly, whores sometimes can be, particularly when they are not taken regularly and have the wit to issue a receipt. But mistresses, it must be added firmly, are not whores. Perhaps it is this vital difference between just supplying sexual favours and supplying the warmth and intimacy of another life in which sexual favours are included that has really caused the demise of the mistress.

My Aunt Beth, bless her, believed her *raison d'être* was to make her man happy. It never occurred to her that this could have made him, in others' eyes, a chauvinist, a selfish pig or an exploiter of women. She desired to please and so she did until she died. Today a woman who simply desires to please, whose life's work is the advancement of pleasure and comfort for a man who should get all that at home is an unenlightened fool who should know better. Her liberated sisters would sooner sweep her under the bed than let her lie on it, and so she has gradually disappeared, retaining only a certain antique value. Pretty soon she will become a collector's item, turning up occasionally in auction rooms to be leapt upon and carted away at great cost by the few that appreciate her. She will probably cost three times the amount she used to when she was a working model, but that is progress for you.

THE DOUBLE-BED COMPANION

'**Any able young Man**, strong in the Back, and endow'd with a good Carnal Weapon, with all the Appurtenances thereunto belonging in good Repair, may have Half A Crown per Night, a Pair of clean Sheets, and other Necessaries, to perform Nocturnal Services upon one Sarah Y——, whose Husband having for these nine Months past lost the use of his Peace-Maker, the unhappy Woman is thereby driven to the last Extremity.'

(*Nottingham Weekly Courant*, 26 November 1717)

'Young **able bodied Gentleman**, the Wants of whose Mind are infinite, whose Soul is elevated and whose Senses refined and capable of Delight, his Desires being thus enlarged for all that promotes Ease, Pleasure and Pomp of Life does consequently require forthwith a comely and ample Serving Wench to share the Sport of his Bed.'

(a Kent Parish News-Sheet, April 1756)

'**ICE AGE WOMAN** lean but not hungry, needs classic vintage man, hungry but not lean, to transport us into sunshine era. Men lacking distinction please do not reply.'

(*Time Out*, 1970)

'**YUMMY BOYS** wanted for breakfast!'

(*Village Voice*, 1975)

'**SLIM**, very attractive "**golf widow**" tired of clubs and balls seeks understanding partner for tee and sympathy. Must have drive, like foreplay and birdies. Good-looking, amusing men welcome.'

(*Forum*, 1980)

'**WIT, WARMTH, PANACHE.** Pretty ivy-educated art consultant, early thirties; vibrant, romantic, charming. Interests: music, theater, travel, architecture, historic preservation, sports, good friends. Seeks successful man 35–50, similar background, interests, urbanity, integrity, with a big cock.'

(*New York Review of Books*, 1983)

'**DAN 34**, OK inside and out, seeks wonderful lover and warm, intelligent female friend – do the two still go together?'

(*Time Out*, 1984)

The Great Snoring Debate or 'If Anyone's Snoring in This Bed it's Not Me!'

I've counted sheep to get to sleep
I've chewed up pills by the billion
I've stood on my head
At the foot of the bed
Till my face went from puce to vermilion
I've brewed up umpteen cups of tea
Relaxed and let my thoughts go free
Is it hot in here – or is it me?
I just can't get to sleep.

I've examined all my deep emotions
Drunk recommended filthy potions
Had a weep
Breathed in deep
Still I just can't get to sleep

But the sobering fact of this story tale is
During all this my favourite male is
Snoring his head off!

A. RAMINI

IT IS A little-known fact of life that in any double bed the one who snores always gets to sleep first. What is more, it is never the snorer who is at fault, but always the snoree who is the one who has to pad off to the kitchen to make a drink, eat an apple, finish off the last of yesterday's trifle and then feel sick and fat for the rest of the night. Always the snorer's partner, never the really guilty party, the habitual snorer. Snorers have it all their own way. You cannot blame them for snoring because they cannot

Thrumph!!
Roar!
Whistle!!

help it and they don't know they are doing it. Prodding them and kicking them and whispering balefully in the night that they are snoring does not help much. They may stop for five minutes, sometimes ten, but that is almost worse. Even the most hardened snoree will lie there, holding his/her breath, just counting the seconds until the inevitable happens and the snoring begins again.

One snoree who was determined that her husband's snoring was not going to destroy her sleep pattern, her peace of mind or her marriage found his snorts and rumbles aroused passions in her she hardly knew she had. As she lay there, kicking, poking and pushing him on his side, his tummy, his face, she began to understand the battered baby syndrome for the first time. She could have battered her husband then and there if it would only stop the snores. What made it worse was that when she finally tape-recorded the horrific noises he made nightly and played them to him the next morning over breakfast he refused to accept that it was actually he who made them.

'No, that's not me. You've amplified it,' he said and nothing would make him change his mind. What is more, like most snorers, he could not or would not try to do anything about it. Eventually she found a brand of French ear-plugs that dulled his rumbling somewhat but even that comparative peace was short-lived, because when the children were tiny she could not wear her ear-plugs for fear of not hearing the baby, and the combination of crying child and snoring husband was almost too much for the marriage to stand. As she paced their bedroom, a whimpering babe in her arms, she longed out loud for him to leave her, to find another woman, to do anything that would make her nights more bearable. He did not do either and she could never take the initiative herself. How could she? She'd feel such a fool, wouldn't she, leaving a man because he snores.

The problem is that we are supposed to be above snoring. It is seen to be something modern couples airily dismiss as unimportant compared to such necessities as a compatible sex-life. Yet how compatible can you be when your lover turns into a snorting, insensitive pig during the tender and vulnerable sleeping hours. It is at moments like these that sex comes a very poor second after a good night's uninterrupted sleep.

Nowadays the snoree's children have grown up and she has discovered more readily available ear-plugs. Without them her marriage would have been yet another snoring casualty, like that of Belinda, a potential snoree I knew, who really loved and admired her snoring lover. She explained to me exactly why she had to turn her back on what might have been a perfect marriage. His snoring, she said with a certain amount of reluctant awe in her voice, was unparalleled. It was not only capable of penetrating walls, in certain areas it could be heard from house to house. What is more, his snoring was of the trumpeting variety (more of this later) which is recognized as the worst kind. There was no friendly whistle or purr in his snore. It rumbled up from his toes right through his body till it was at last released, triumphantly through both nose and mouth at the same time. My shattered friend tried everything. Ear-plugs, pilows over the head (hers rather than his, although there were moments . . .), making him sleep on his belly. Nothing was even half successful. She tried getting mindlessly drunk so that nothing, not even the will of the devil could wake her, but all that happened was that she was sick, and as her vomiting was even worse than his snoring that ploy was abandoned. Her last brave try was when they both decided that perhaps the double bed could be used for sexual pleasure only and the two would sleep apart at opposite ends of the house.

This was sadly abandoned as any experienced double-bed user could have predicted. Double beds are not simply sexual arenas and if treated that way they lose their charm very rapidly indeed. And so the snorer won yet again. My friend who never did find a partner as charming and wonderful except in that one vital area is still single while her snoring ex-lover has happily settled down with the ideal wife. She's deaf.

What is the charm do you suppose
About a man who picks his nose?
Who scratches at his private parts
And, worse than this,
Who farts?

Who could be spouse of such a prize
An angel in suburban guise?
But no, curtail your swift applause.
The truth is
The wife indoors snores.

Once a snoree has accepted the fact that a snoring partner is going to be a fixture of double-bed life then he or she must also face the fact that the list of ways to handle snorers is depressingly short. The first and probably most popular method is called 'Giving In'.

A Giver-in does not bother with the brewing up of drinks to be drunk alone at the kitchen table in the cold when the heating has gone off. Nor does the Giver-in bother too much with kicking and poking and piercing whispers about how the quality of snoring is on a level with the rumblings of Vesuvius before a particularly lethal eruption. A Giver-in simply climbs out of the double bed and spends the rest of the night, fitfully, on the spare single or the sofa. Some poor despairing souls have been known to resort to a few odd pillows, the picnic rug and the floor. Even if they are lucky enough actually to have another bed to fall into, snorees rarely enjoy a complete and restful night's sleep. Somehow the guilt of sleeplessness is theirs, and they spend the rest of the night tossing about in a sea of bedclothes. The worst part about Giving In is that the Giver-in, in order to retain any kind of togetherness, has to creep out of the double, making sure the snorer is not disturbed (fat chance!) and later on in the early hours creep back again. The reason for this is as we have already noted.

Double beds are made for two cosy people and if they become not only unshared but seen to be unshared they begin to lose their point . . . What is more once the Giver-in has settled for this role, the guilt does not stop there. There are also the silent 'how-could-you?' looks to cope with over the breakfast because snorers are never at fault. Snoring, we have to accept, is rather like contraception. The one who has it done to them, like sex, is the one who has to do something about it. So a woman takes the pill, gets sterilized, uses an IUD and the snoree buys the ear-plugs, sleeps in the single, does not sleep at all. Sad but true. Hence we observe the scene of the snorer enjoying a hearty breakfast of bacon, eggs, toast and marmalade, albeit accompanied by the silent disapproval of his/her mate who has let a little thing like a few snores disrupt the matrimonial couch, while the snoree, eyes like pee-holes in the snow, makes do with a little black coffee and a de-fizzed alka seltzer.

None of this escaped the keen eye of American humorist, Ogden Nash, when he wrote: 'A husband is a man who two minutes after his head touches the pillow is snoring like an overloaded omnibus. Particularly on those occasions when between the humidity and the mosquitoes your own bed is no longer a bed, but an insomnibus.'

But Givers-in who complain and do nothing have no one but themselves to blame, because nowadays they could exert a little pressure and try ploy two, which is known as: Having-it-seen-to. This occurs when the snoree recognizes emotionally as well as intellectually that the snorer is not actually snoring every night out of spite and really cannot help him/herself. Sometimes it is little more than a medical problem like leprosy or haemorrhoids. In this case all that is required is a small nasal operation and hey presto! No more snoring! Having-it-seen-to is particularly applicable to wives of sportsmen, because pushing your nose out of joint on the football pitch or in the boxing ring is practically compulsory during undergraduate life and nine out of ten of the muddy, muscley men rushing about beating hell out of each other in the name of sport snore their heads off thanks to the overenthusiasm of their opponents and team-mates. So when a wife takes him aside saying she has got a bone to pick with her active sportsman more often than not it is the one blocking his nasal passages. One woman who had her husband seen-to swears that they would never have started a family if he had not had his nose done; which does not show an unusual confusion about where babies come from, but simply proves that his snoring was keeping them apart rather dramatically.

The third ploy which demands a somewhat placid and easy-going personality is called 'Making-the-best-of-it'. Makers-of-the-best-of-it are pleasant and charming souls who apply themselves to the whole many-faceted subject of snoring. They make lists in their heads about how often and when the snoring occurs; they compare with similarly affected friends all the different types of snoring that exist and make quite a hobby of it. I have to underline here that this kind of Maker-of-the-best-of-it is fairly rare and probably a dying breed (owing to not enough sleep). But it is them we have to thank for the comprehensive catalogue we can turn to on snorers and the variety of noises they make.

Interestingly a snoree does not have to be married to a snorer in order to take the blame.

'We made a pact,' my friend told me. 'All of us in the party had to take turns at sharing with D.V. Throughout the trip he never knew why his room-mate kept changing. No one had the heart to tell him.' As I have previously observed, the snorer is never at fault.

Having decided what type of snorer is theirs to bear or cope with, potential snorees can either choose any of the three better-known ploys ('Give-in', 'Have-it-seen-to' or 'Make-the-best-of-it') or devise a personal method. There are many of these ranging from emptying cold water all over the snorer's head, which is unsuccessful in the long run as it is always the snoree who has to clean up afterwards, through to murder. This device has not actually been documented but many a snoree has been known to nod his/her head wisely implying private knowledge of such an event.

In between these extreme measures are more historical remedies which some swear by and some swear at. The British in Victorian times believed that as long as you could get a snorer on his/her side the snoring would stop. This is undoubtedly true with many a part-time snorer but as any hardened snoree will vouchsafe makes little or no difference to the kind of snorers described here. It is worth trying however. What the Victorians used to do was prop the snorer in a fixed side position with a bolster or two. (Readers who are too young to have heard of bolsters should understand they are a type of long, tubular pillow that stretches from one side of the bed to the other. They rarely appear these days, except in smart French hotels, which is a pity as they had a multitude of uses ranging from

1) THE TRUMPETER

The best-known and most prevalent snorer. Also considered one of the worst for the snoree, the Trumpeter inhales an enormous amount of air, holds on to it for an exasperating number of seconds before letting loose loudly and triumphantly with an enormous trumpeting sound. Some snorees maintain that the trumpeter quite often does not keep up the snoring for as long as some of the other varieties, owing to eventual exhaustion. Others maintain that this is wishful thinking.

2) THE WHISTLER

The whistler starts off quite low and for half an hour at least the snoree can be fooled into thinking it is not going to get worse than heavy, shrill breathing. This is rarely the case. The Whistler builds up gradually but relentlessly and after a while sounds like a good imitation of a steam engine.

3) THE TRUMPETING-WHISTLER/ WHISTLING-TRUMPETER

Another common variety successfully combines the two best-known snores into one monster snore. The whistling usually precedes the trumpeting on a regular basis. Sometimes the whistling is only intermittent, punctuating the trumpeting on infrequent occasions. This type is not a new variety but is still categorized as a Whistling Trumpeter.

4) THE PROLONGED SIGH

I am not convinced that this variety is accurately labelled, because it was described to me by the snorer's mother who knew the snore well but never had to share a bed with it. When it was imitated for me, with feeling, by the snoree it sounded less like a prolonged sigh than an air-raid warning. A little known snore. Needs further research.

5) THE RUMBLER

Sometimes confused with the Trumpeter, the Rumbler is a little-known snore with a wealth of variations. The low Rumbler sounds like a motor bike with a deep pitch; the common or garden middle-range Rumbler has been likened to a tractor in some reports and a vacuum cleaner in others, while the high-pitched Rumbler sounds like a cheap lawnmower. Like most cheap lawnmowers it never actually gets into gear but just chugs and rumbles in a distinctively irritating way. The only possible advantage the Rumbler snoree has over her/his fellow snorees is that on occasions the Rumbler can make a sound that is somehow comforting. I found this hard to believe until I was told the tale of one Rumbler (in his wakeful state a most meek and mild sort of man, like Clark Kent), who became a veritable superman in his sleep, rumbling away in such a 'macho' fashion that a would-be burglar on hearing the low-pitched rumble turned tail and disappeared rather than tangle with him.

6) THE SNORTER
Not totally accepted by the dyed-in-the-wool snoring fraternity, the Snorter emits a strange pig-like noise suddenly and intermittently. While trumpeting and whistling snorees may treat a snorting snoree with some derision, maintaining that he/she is lucky, it should be pointed out that living with a Snorter is no bed of roses either. After all, who would choose to go to bed with a pig?

7) THE GLOTTAL STOP
This snore is more restful for the snoree than many of the other varieties as it can never be quite as loud as, for instance, the Trumpeter or the Prolonged Sigh. It begins in the usual way with the elongated intake of breath accompanied by a deep snort, but instead of the whistle or trumpeting sound this snore ends, rather charmingly, with a 'ping' – not shrill, not harsh, but a ping nevertheless resulting in a glottal-stop effect. It is this snore that most snorees would choose to go to bed with if they ever had anything as luxurious as a choice in these matters.

8) THE DORMANT VOLCANO
This is a common or garden snore that has the distinction of convincing snorees that they are the only ones who have ever been subjected to it. This is because of its special vibratory quality, not so much noisy as physical. It is not unusual for a Dormant Volcano snoree to describe the whole room as shaking or vibrating.

'It's like sleeping,' they say, 'with Mount Etna', or 'Stromboli', or, depending on their knowledge of volcanoes, 'Popocatépetl'.

One Dormant Volcano snoree described a bird-watching trip through China as a snoring nightmare. He had spent a great deal of money in order to travel around eastern Mongolia with a party of eminent bird-watchers. Unfortunately there is no such thing as a single room in China and he was obliged to share a bedroom. During the day his room-mate was a brilliant ornithologist, one of the foremost authorities on Chinese waterfowl. At night he became a Dormant Volcano. The transformation had more than a hint of the Doctor Jekyll and Mr Hyde about it.

'The room actually shook,' my friend marvelled, with a certain awe in his voice. 'Things on the bedside table rattled!'

snorer-propping to pretending to be sleeping bodies when the real bodies were doing something else entirely — a well-known ploy at country house weekends. Bolsters were so useful in fact that the verb 'to bolster' — one's ego, personality, leg — remains in common parlance while the bolster itself is a dying commodity.) Depending on the size of the double bed this method leaves little room for the snoree to sleep, but with the king-size doubles fashionable today, it could just work.

Other particularly nasty anti-snoring devices included the attachment of a leather thong to the bedpost into which the unfortunate snorer was expected to put his/her upper arm. The idea behind this specialized torture was that the snorer could not turn on his/her back and therefore could not snore. He/she also could not sleep which made the thong as an anti-snoring device one hundred per cent effective. I have also had the 'snore ball' brought to my attention. This was apparently attached to the back of the pyjamas and squeaked on impact, rather like a child's toy, immediately waking both the snorer and snoree. Neither of these devices seem to have found their market.

The Victorian snoree also used to pinch the snorer's nose. I recommended this method to one desperate snoree who reported next morning that it certainly stopped the snoring, but at what cost! Her husband was in a particularly deep sleep at the time and the shock of having his air supply cut off made him thrash out in an extremely lethal fashion.

'He let out an almighty yell. His arms flailed about and he kicked so suddenly that he broke the table lamp and the glass of water I'd put beside it for my sleeping pill.' He also broke her will. She will never pinch his nose again.

Research has not unearthed any other specially suitable historical method, although I have heard rumour of an Edwardian Snoring Bonnet, supposedly invented by some wag at the court of Edward VII of England. This sounds highly unlikely to me and I am inclined to think it is simply an invention of some superior television quiz master.

If a snoree really wishes to take advice from history he/she could listen to Dr James Graham, who had plenty to say in 1775 on the subject of men and women sharing a bed at all:

Apparatus to prevent snoring [1871]

There is not in my opinion anything in nature which is more immediately calculated totally to subject health, strength, love and esteem and indeed everything that is desirable in the married state than that odious, most indelicate and most hurtful custom of man and wife continually pigging together in one and the same bed. Nothing more unwise, nothing more indecent, nothing more unnatural than for a man and woman to sleep and snore and steam and do everything else that's indelicate together three hundred and sixty-five times every year.

And it is only because we will insist on 'pigging' together that we have this snoring problem at all. It is odd though how rarely even the most despairing snorees will desert the double bed permanently. They may wish to choke their snoring partners, smother them, pull their ears until their eyes water. They will even spend much of most nights in a separate single bed but they disdain any suggestion of deserting the double bed completely. We like double beds. We like sharing them, and if our partners snore we just stiffen our upper lips — and wish despairingly that our snoring partners would do likewise with their lower ones.

Double Beds for Second-Timers

'Love is wonderful and more comfortable the second time around.'
JOHNNY MERCER

You would think that once marriage had been tried and found to fail the disappointed participant in the game of wedlock would give up, go home and leave that particular arena to other players. 'Oh well,' a divorcee might say, 'why buy a book when you can join a library?' – or words to that effect – and proceed to have lots of sparkling affairs and never think about marriage again. But it does not work that way.

'I can stand the dressing up and the relentless sexiness of an affair for so long,' explained one divorcee on the eve of a second marriage, 'but there comes a time when you want to leave off your girdle, forget the mascara and go to bed with a bowl of corn-flakes. And if you can do that with a man for God's sake marry him. You can't fart in an affair.'

There you have it. Marriage is relaxing. As Mrs Patrick Campbell said: 'Ah, the deep, deep peace of the double bed after the hurly burly of the chaise longue.' Wedlock may be stultifying, but at least it is peaceful. It may be confining, but it is also protective. Men and women are God's optimists. Often more foolish than lemmings, sometimes much blinder than bats, we of the human race take the biscuit for disregarding the obvious and doing what we want no matter what happens to us. Hence second-timers; or third or fourth or fifth. 'Second-timers' are those who will try again. A great many of them try again a great many times but they, for the purposes of this book, also fall into this category.

Second-timers are not looking for the mere gratification of sexual urges, nor are they carried away solely with the thought of romance. Most of us – first-, second- and old-timers – have looked for both several times during our lives and have found that a glorious, abandoned affair, relentlessly sexy, fills that particular bill perfectly.

Affairs are wonderful. They put a spring in the step and a sparkle in the eye. They are magical things that everyone deserves to experience at least once. The mistake too many people make is in pretending the affairs are built to last. They are not. Like any other magic trick, love affairs lose their charm if they last long enough for us to see how they work. Once an affair looks as though it will turn into a relationship it is doomed. The difference between affairs and relationships could be likened to the difference between lingerie and underwear: affairs are camiknickers; relationships are Y-fronts. First-timers could be said to fill their bottom drawers with lingerie and as it wears out replace it with underwear; old-timers to keep certain bits of lingerie as collector's items; second-timers to have a drawerful of underwear with a pile of lingerie in the corner, and the really successful second-timer to replace worn-out underwear with lingerie.

It is not easy to see why marriage continues to attract the majority of people most of the time, particularly today when the whole idea of wedlock is dismissed daily in the popular press. On top of all these essays in sociology are the true propagandists, the humorists who have always found marriage great copy. Oscar Wilde naturally had plenty to say including: 'In married life three is company and two are none', while much later the American humorist Jean Kerr said: 'Marrying a man is like buying something you've been admiring for a long time in a shop window. You may love it when you get home but it doesn't always go with everything else in the house.'

The film star Shelley Winters, a second-timer in the wider sense, said: 'In Hollywood all marriages are happy. It's trying to live together afterwards that causes problems.' While Adela St John, a wickedly funny American columnist, believed that second-timers have merely taken the first step. 'Every woman,' she said, 'is entitled to a middle husband she can forget.' Such cynicism bodes ill for second-time success but James Garner, the American actor who, incidentally, will not go within spitting distance of Hollywood if he can help it, said recently: 'Marriage is like the army. Everyone complains but you'd be surprised how many people re-enlist.'

Second-timers, more than any other double-bed category, need special care and consideration. Unlike first-timers who have not got around to it and old-timers who got around to it a lifetime ago, second-timers almost always have appendages in the form of children. This condition in its most lavish form is often known as 'Yours, Mine and Ours'. As is obvious, any household containing a version of 'Yours, Mine and Ours' has to have at the very least three children. This can be a blessing, though not all the time. As the redoubtable Mrs Gaskell wrote in *Wives and Daughters*: 'To be sure, a stepmother to a girl is a different thing to a second wife to a man.' It is no coincidence that a great deal of traditional children's literature is based on the character of the wicked stepmother who spent every waking hour making her pathetic little stepchildren's lives living hell.

Joan Crawford, dressed to kill but not for bed: RONALD GRANT COLLECTION

Remember poor little Cinderella who crouched barefoot and tousled in the corner of her wicked stepmother's kitchen, only good enough to clean the house and stitch finery for her ugly sisters until her fingers bled. Cinderella's stepmother undoubtedly had the double bed firmly in control; otherwise how could she have got away with such nasty behaviour? Then there were those two poor little mites Hansel and Gretel, who were deliberately lost — and not just by their wicked stepmother, but by their own father who sired them. We can only suppose that the woman who supplanted Hansel and Gretel in their father's affections was a female to be reckoned with, particularly in the double-bed department.

Today, we may be thankful, there is also a certain amount written about how the pathetic little children make their stepmothers' lives a living hell but tradition dies hard and besides, why shouldn't the dear little thing have a Cadillac for her sixteenth birthday if she really wants one. It is therefore vital to keep the double bed sacrosanct. One couple I knew insisted that there was nothing like humble petroleum jelly for this purpose. It took me some time to find a way of asking why, and I was eventually rewarded by the eminently sensible reply: 'We put it on the door handle to keep the kids out.' It was a brilliant move. Actually *locking* the door would spell out that these second-timers did not want the little dears, the petroleum jelly only implied it.

Unfortunately, petroleum jelly as a deterrent has only a limited lifespan and phase two in 'making us all one big happy family' is in the decision of whether the children should be allowed in the double bed, how often, and if so whether the bed should be an emperor super size. To those who are merely contemplating second-timer life or who have not even got that far, such a question may seem banal. If they had ever had to confront it they would realize its profound importance. The whole future of the marriage could depend upon it.

'If we let them in will we ever be alone?' says one partner.

'If we keep them out will they feel rejected?' says the other.

'If we let them in and get a bigger bed will they think we're sex maniacs?'

'If we keep a reasonable-sized double bed and still let them in will we ever know a comfortable night again?'

As with any question of consequence there is no one correct answer. The wretched second-timers who opt for the huge double bed will leave themselves bereft of any logical reason to refuse to have the whole family in bed with them all the time. If, on the other hand, the children do not want to climb into their bed the choice of a vast double seems slightly obscene. Then there is a whole panoply of arguments against the purchase of a smallish double bed, including: it looks mean; it is not substantial; and even if you really want to be squashed up together you can achieve that in the privacy of a decently sized double bed. The discussion can continue indefinitely and threaten the second-timers' chances of success.

Whatever is decided as to size and grandeur, there is no doubt about one thing: the double bed of the second marriage must never be inherited from the first. It is an interesting sidelight on the role of the double bed that, once a first marriage has been dissolved and a new partner has been chosen to replace the faulty one, the first stick of furniture to be found wanting is the bed. A new spouse will quite happily eat off the first husband's china or carve the joint with the first husband's silver; his shirt will tumble about in the same washing machine; but he will no more sleep in his predecessor's bed than fly. Even when it is rather a nice bed, of the right size, style and inner-sprung firmness new partners (men never and women rarely) accept the bed that went before. Perhaps the fact that the double bed and the happier moments of the first marriage go together has something to do with it; perhaps in spite of our veneer of civilization we do believe in ghosts and spirits and the aura of pleasanter, sexier times. Nine times out of ten the double bed is treated like its previous owner — replaced.

It seems desperately unfair that second-timers should be subject to niggardly little fears about the-bed-that-was, because no other double-bed group has more to cope with and more to overcome. Rarely, as we have seen, is a second-time pairing about only two people. Even if there are no children by either previous marriage there are friends, relatives, even in-laws who have become important enough to be retained in the new life. One second-time wife I knew found herself faced with not just one mother-in-law but two. And it was mother-in-law number one, who was not actually related to anyone in the new family, who moved in. Her only son had died leaving her daughter-in-law a widow. Where else could 'mother' go?

Worse than this by far is the guilt and disruption of divorce. Time and time again we are told that the ease with which we discard one partner and take on another is a despicable invention of the twentieth century. The indissolubility of marriage, the duration and durability of the institution until our present time is, we have been told, a historical fact. No wonder second-timers have to be such optimists. They have believed for so long they are such failures. But William Ferdinand Mount, in his book *The Subversive Family*, points out quite clearly that:

> *The most regular and universal feature of non-Christian or pre-Christian marriage was the relative ease of divorce . . . what marks out the Christian era from earlier and later times is the insistence that marriage should invariably be till death us do part. It is this which makes the dramatic contrast with the marriage customs of virtually all the people who were to be Christianized over the centuries, the Romans no less than the Anglo Saxons, the Celts in the Dark Ages no less than most of the inhabitants of Africa and Asia who were to be converted by missionaries a thousand years later. Only the Hindus seem to have maintained anything like the strictness of the Catholic Church towards divorce.*

The most famous, and in the light of this new research, possibly the most misunderstood second-timer in history was King Henry VIII of England. Like so many second-timers he found he just could not get it right and tried again, not just once, but as everyone knows, five times, never with resounding success. If he had just relaxed and been satisfied with his mistresses fewer heads would have rolled but unfortunately Henry VIII suffered the second-timer's disease, the search for respectability.

In addition to that problem, he had to produce a male heir, and it was the pursuit of the elusive son that drove him, restlessly, from bed to bed. His wish was gratified when Jane Seymour gave birth to Edward, but Jane died and the boy was always sickly. So Henry continued his quest.

Henry, like his father, Henry VII, attached great significance to the ritual of the bedchamber. Indeed Henry VII had one of his ushers, known as a 'Squire of the Body' cast holy water on the bed from a gold cachet to thwart the demons and frighten off evil spirits. Henry VIII, whom papists considered not much better than an evil spirit himself after his break with

Rome, did not go quite that far, but his ceremony of the bedchamber was a formal, ritualistic affair that required the services of twelve men: two grooms, two pages of the wardrobe, two 'Squires of the Body' and six yeomen.

Security was of paramount importance and it was one yeoman's job to approach the straw mattress of the bed with a dagger and fiercely stab it from top to bottom in case something or someone was concealed there. It was then up to another yeoman to lay a further mattress on top, which was searched in turn by yet another loyal servant of the king. Finally a groom was left with a torch to light the bed until his Royal Majesty decided to enter it. Undoubtedly King Henry VIII, like other royal personages up to the early nineteenth century, treated the ceremony of the bed as just that, a ceremony which, once completed, left him free to visit any other beds he fancied. The ritual of the bed was of vital importance in the life of the court, and some of the ancient titles still remain. The present Queen of England still has her Mistress of the Bedchamber.

Today the British royal family is one of the last great bastions of first-timerism, although a small crack has appeared with the divorce of HRH Princess Margaret and Lord Snowdon. He has, of course, remarried and is now one of a select band of near-royal second-timers. But the most dazzlingly successful in the second-timer division is HRH Princess Michael of Kent. Princess Michael, previously Marie Christine von Reibnitz, born in Czechoslovakia and brought up in Australia, was formerly married to a nice, understanding British merchant banker, Tom Troubridge. The divorce was fairly amicable as divorces go, and Marie Christine and Prince Michael were married with a minimum of fuss in Vienna in 1978. In order to marry a Catholic and a divorcee Prince Michael had to renounce his right to the throne that could have been his if the nineteen people in front of him had died. However, Prince and Princess Michael are no different from all true second-timers, who seem to ache for respectability and seek to erase all memory of any previous love. Princess Michael could not be properly happy until she was married in a Catholic church just as if her first marriage had never really happened. For five years the Pope refused to grant the young Kents the necessary dispensation but then in 1983 he finally relented and after a ceremony in the cardinal's private chapel in Westminster Cathedral Princess Michael of Kent became the whitest second-timer of them all.

Catherine Deneuve playing the bored French housewife who sold herself on empty afternoons in <u>Belle de Jour</u>, 1967: RONALD GRANT COLLECTION

Although we can understand why those who enter the royal circle may wish to remain pure and unblemished in the eyes of the world it is more difficult to see why a fallen angel like Elizabeth Taylor still wishes to don the respectable cloak of marriage every time. If she marries her current fiancé (at the time of writing, Victor Luna) he will bring her tally up to eight which does make each new protestation of deep and undying love somewhat tarnished. Even her husbands have found her need to be married slightly extraordinary. The late Richard Burton, who distinguished himself by marrying her twice, would have been quite happy to have had a dazzling, impossible affair – or even two – but, as he once said, 'Elizabeth needs to be married.'

Second-timers, both famous and otherwise, share a profound belief that each love is both the first and the last and must therefore be made legal. Among the great scandals of early nineteenth-century Europe were the affairs of the Honourable Jane Digby, who was brought up in Holkham Hall, Norfolk and who died in Damascus, wife of a great sheikh. Jane Digby became Lady Ellenborough then Baroness Veningen, then Countess Theotky and finally the wife of Sheikh Abdul Medjuel El Mezrab – and they were only her legal masters. She was the archetypal second-timer, pursuing love and life with the kind of innocent enthusiasm only virgins are thought to show.

Jane was a great horsewoman and a restless traveller, but not even she moved anywhere without the equipment befitting a lady of her station, which included her silver, her linen and, of course, her bed. When she was in her sixties and married at last to her demanding and exciting sheikh, Jane Digby El Mezrab was a living monument to the agelessness of the second-timer and the delights of double-bed life. Isobel Burton, wife of the explorer Sir Richard Burton and an accurate if gushing diarist wrote: 'She looked splendid in Oriental dress and if you saw her in the bazaar you would have said she was not more than thirty-four years of age.' Jane herself wrote on her birthday: 'Sixty-two years of age and an impetuous romantic girl of seventeen cannot exceed me in ardent passionate feelings.' What a tribute to the joy of love and sex and what a slap in the eye for the so-called inevitable onslaught of old age!

It may not seem entirely fair to all the charming first-timers of the world, who as individuals are probably as sexy and as fascinating as can be, to say that most of the really glamorous women in history were either immoral or second-timers or both, but it does seem to be true. From Cleopatra to Helen of Troy, from Ingrid Bergman to the Duchess of Windsor or Elizabeth Taylor, the heroines who make our hearts miss a beat and our spirits sing are the second-timers, who give recklessly and shamelessly and then when passion is spent and the marriage is dead rise joyously to do the whole thing all over again. First-timers who become old-timers together may stare disapprovingly, tut-tutting at the ease with which second-timers forget the sacred vows of marriage, but they just do not see it that way. For them, the poet John Dryden summed it all up when he wrote:

Why should a foolish marriage vow
Which long ago was made,
Oblige us to each other now
When passion is decayed?
We loved, and we loved, as long as we could,
Till our love was loved out in us both:
But our marriage is dead, when the pleasure is fled:
'Twas pleasure first made it an oath.

JOHN DRYDEN

Insomnia and Other Related Ills

'Couldn't sleep and wouldn't sleep
Until I could sleep where I shouldn't sleep,
'Bewitched, bothered and bewildered am I.'

'PAL JOEY', RODGERS/HART

UNREQUITED LOVE, LUST, passion – call it what you will – is still one of the best reasons for running out of sleep. Is there anyone in the world over the age of sixteen who has not gone to bed, heart a-quiver, pulse racing, determined to erase all memories of yesterday's lover, only to toss and turn until the first crack of dawn signals the onslaught of a troubled fitful sleep before they wake again, feeling as if their eyes had been made up from the

inside and their teeth had gone hairy? Who has not spent subsequent nights indulging in those secret, unspoken conversations between self and the other self, lying there composing brilliant, succinct sentences that would cut their faithless lovers to the quick if only they could hear? And who has not taken the telephone beside the bed during the composition of these dignified exchanges just in case it should ring and the faithless one be there . . . Who has not?

The poet Shelley once wrote how 'love itself slumbers on', which it may well, but alas the unfortunate lovers do not. Nor do their long-suffering friends, because the step after the private conversation in the dark is the less private one conducted either by telephone or over the kitchen table, when a good friend proves just what a good friend is by listening deep into the night to the interminable confidences of the stricken lover.

The terrible fact about losing sleep over a broken love affair is that one does not learn by experience. As one lovelorn friend remarked, 'Each time it happens I swear I'll never venture on that precipice again and a few weeks later there I go, all shining innocence and wide-eyed trust straight to the cliff and over the top.' There is an inevitability about it all, perfectly expressed by Edna St Vincent Millay when she wrote: 'Life isn't one damned thing after another. It's the same damn thing over and over again.'

Alas, there is no known cure for the sleeplessness that goes with a diagnosed dose of bruised-heartitis, except what barmen crudely term 'the hair of the dog'. But perhaps those of us who crave love, and that is all of us, would miss the bittersweet pain that is an obligatory ingredient of true lovesickness. Lorenz Hart, who wrote some of the wittiest and most apposite lyrics in the 1930s, summed up our basic streak of masochism when he made Judy Garland and Mickey Rooney sing:

'The sleepless nights,
'The daily fights,
'The quick toboggan when you reach the heights,.
I miss the kisses and I miss the fights,
I wish I were in love again.

and:

'The furtive sigh,
'The blackened eye,
'The words I'll love you till the day I die,
'The self-deception that believes the lie,
I wish I were in love again.

'I WISH I WERE IN LOVE AGAIN',
RODGERS/HART

Insomnia that is not caused by a broken heart or a snoring partner or anything you can actually put your finger on is the worst kind of all – and the most commonplace. The American humorist James Thurber, who claimed he always suffered from the lack of a good night's sleep, maintained that we unfortunates who live in the twentieth century suffer from the four 'A's: Anxiety, Apprehension, Agonizing and Aspirin. His fellow humorist Ogden Nash might have said it had nothing to do with the twentieth century but went much further back than that. 'I am certain,' he wrote, 'that the first words of the Sleeping Beauty to her Prince were: "You *would* have to kiss me just when I had dropped off after tossing and turning for a hundred years." ' You would think it would be made easier if insomniacs married each other and spent the small hours counting sheep together or sipping jointly from a loving cup of vallium, but it does not happen that way. You know how it is. There is the belle of the ball and there is the party pooper and they are invariably married to each other. In the same way there are larks who waken gladly as dawn's first tentative finger reaches into the sky, and there are owls who consider daybreak obscene. They too inevitably marry each other creating mayhem in their married lives, with one blissfully asleep and the other merely wishing he/she was. Even on the rare occasions when owl marries owl, it is not a howling success either. Both maintain, with murderous glance, that neither had a wink of sleep and that the other snored his/her head off. The truth is that both woke and both slept, but never simultaneously. It is, as greater philosophers than I have observed, a cruel world.

Not the least of the cruel aspects of insomnia is the fact that those who sleep like logs and never lose a night's sleep cannot begin to understand what it is like. It is said that President Truman slept like a baby no matter what was going on in Hiroshima and could not understand what his aides were complaining about when they appeared limp from exhaustion and lack of sleep in the Oval Office in the morning. As one insomniac described the problem, 'Insomnia is like being deaf. Other people can't see anything to commiserate over – so they don't.' And there it is. The blind are pitied, the lame are helped, but an insomniac – or worse, a *deaf* insomniac – has no hope.

Luckily for insomniacs, their fellow sufferers have had to find *something* to do with the fearsome waking hours somewhere between midnight and dawn, and a great many of them have spent their time gainfully employed devising remedies to ward off the perils of sleepless-ness. They range from hypnosis which sounds good but has flaws, not the least of which is 'where can you find a hypnotist to do house visits at 2 a.m.?', through to pretending you *have* to get up in ten minutes and will just grab an extra five minutes' sleep. In the middle range there are extremely sensible suggestions such as 'make love'. You do not get to sleep but at least you enjoy your waking hours. This sounds good, always supposing that your partner is also awake and interested in such suggestions and not, like Ogden Nash's Sleeping Beauty, going to nag you till dawn if you so much as kiss her/him.

James Thurber, who was one of this century's great insomniacs, came up with wonderfully complicated word games in which insomniacs keep themselves amused playing with words and reciting them backwards. According to Mr Thurber, you often come up with a word that is a far better description of what it is describing than its original. Take for instance 'ping-pong'. 'Ping-pong,' wrote Thurber, 'a trade name for table tennis, was presumably selected for its supposed onomatopoeic effect, but I submit that 'gnop-gnip' is much more successful, that it really sounds like the game in progress.' This is so obviously true that any curious insomniac could hardly resist having a stab at some of his/her favourite sports to check how they would turn out. Hence 'golf', a game of much frustration becomes 'flog', which is exactly how most golf games turn out. 'Football' becomes 'llabtoof', which has a certain Welsh charm in the double-L and the traditional difficulty of pronunciation. 'Badminton' becomes 'notnimdab', which is not nim dab description at all. 'Yekcoh' describes precisely how some people feel about hockey, to be shortened after usage has become familiar to 'yek!', and so it goes on.

After spelling words backwards, you can progress to 'spoonerisms' which are accomplished by interchanging the first letters of different words. Thus 'mum' and 'dad' becomes 'dum' and 'mad' (as well they might if they indulge too heavily in spoonerisms). 'A little house' becomes a 'hittle louse', a 'well-earned drink' is a 'dell-earned wink'. A favourite insomniac ploy is to take a well-known and well-loved story such as *Goldilocks and the Three Bears* or *Loldigocks and the Bee Threars* and play with it. So you have 'Bather Fear' (pronounced 'Barther Fare') baying salefully, 'Booze wheen bleeping in my sled?' and 'laughty nittle Loldigocks' climbing out of Father Bear's bed because it was 'hoo tard and boo tig and rot night at all'.

An automatic fan invented by J.B. Williamson of Louisville, Kentucky (1872).
The moving strips were to cool the air and drive away insects

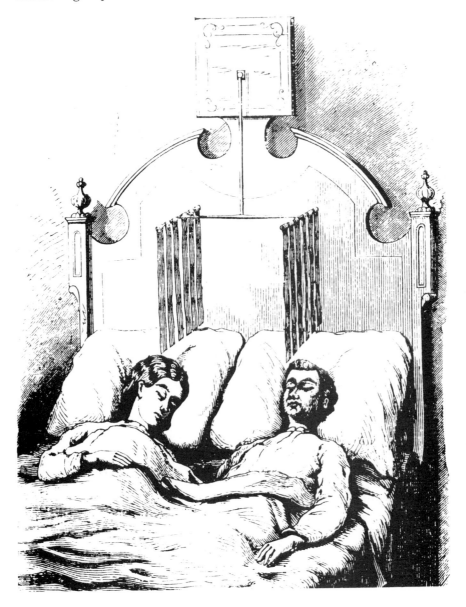

Insomniacs of a more literary bent may prefer something more erudite, for example the well-known Coleridge verse on sleep:

Oh Sleep, it is a gentle thing
'Beloved from pole to pole.
'To Mary Queen the praise be given!
She sent the gentle sleep from heaven,
'That slid into my soul.

which becomes:

So Leep! It is a thentle ging,
leboved prom fole po tole,
Mo 'Tary 'Preen the quraise ge biven!
Se shent the slentle geep hom freaven
Shlat tid into sy moul.

Surely the best way to combat insomnia is to confront it head on. Insomniacs who insist on taking themselves up to bed at an early hour, in order to catch whatever sleep is available, are asking for trouble. It is one thing to lie in a darkened room, wracked with anxiety by interminable wakefulness when the rest of the world slumbers. But to lie in a darkened room, while others are still watching television, reading or doing something really interesting is madness. As Dorothy Parker pointed out, 'Bed before eleven, nuts before seven.'

The real trick must be refusing to accept that being awake when everyone else is sleeping is necessarily a bad thing. After all, if there is no hard and fast law that everybody has to sleep for at least six hours at a stretch between midnight and dawn, then there is *no such thing as insomnia*. I realize that those who have spent most of their adult life fighting for sleep will find this observation not only cruel and heartless, but silly as well. But it is true that there is no such thing as a normal night's sleep. All of us have different sleep patterns, and require varying amounts. Practically every child-care expert you care to name, from Doctor Spock to Doctor Zeuss, has pointed out that although you can *try* this way or that of turning an owlet into a baby lark, you will be defeated. In the old days there were old wives to blame for silly pronouncements such as 'seven hours' sleep for a man, eight for a woman and nine for a fool'. Today we have psychologists who make equally annoying statements such as, 'insomniacs are frightened of sleep because they are frightened of death'. There may be a grain of truth in both statements; perhaps there are some non-sleepers who are scared of dying, just as there are some women who need eight hours' sleep. But there are also some women who need six or four or ten hours' sleep and some insomniacs who lie wishing for death (*anything* to break the sleepless monotony).

The fact that sleep in long, delicious stretches eludes insomniacs should not be cause for brow-beating or soul-searching. Rather than wasting those midnight hours, make use of them. Writers often find they write better, more clearly with less dross and waffle if they work at night, wrapped in the blanket of silence a sleeping household brings. If the typewriter is too noisy or the hand that holds the pen too weary, then read.

'The Nightmare': Henry Fuseli, 1741–1825. GIFT OF MR AND MRS BERT L. SMOKLER AND MR AND MRS LAWRENCE A. FLEISCHMAN, DETROIT INSTITUTE OF ARTS

Do not choose light-hearted reading matter designed to get you to sleep, but demanding stuff: research material perhaps, or a book you have been keeping as a treat for yourself. Make yourself comfortable. If you feel like a drink and a slice of cherry cake, have some. Why not? A friend who calls himself a reformed insomniac sleeps as little as he ever did. The difference is that now he enjoys his sleeplessness. 'Nothing tastes nicer,' he says, 'than a slice of not-quite-cold beef picked from last night's dinner. Or a cool roast potato. Delicious.' The charm of these midnight feasts is that they are not very grown-up and therefore enormously pleasurable. And there is no one to tick you off about picking. There are disadvantages, of course, such as, 'isn't all this terribly fattening?'

'Nonsense,' says my friend. 'Food is only fattening when other people see you eating it,' which sounds like another old wives' tale to me, but at least this old wife is on our side.

Other recommendations include keeping a bowl of apples beside the bed to chew at while working deep into the night. It should be added that this was suggested by a bachelor who may have shared his double bed on an occasional basis but never as a long-term arrangement. The point is that, no matter how each individual works out his/her plan, the end result must be in seeing those sleepless hours in exactly the same light as any others in the available twenty-four. Just because they come up between two and four-thirty in the morning instead of two and four-thirty in the afternoon does not make then unusable. They do not have to be wasted.

It would be nice to report that having adopted this philosophy, users have found that lack of anxiety has brought sleep as its true reward. Unfortunately this does not seem to be the case. You will probably get as little sleep as before but at least it will not worry you to death. It is just that the heavy sleepers of this world outnumber the light sleepers. It is yet another win for the silent majority, although the reason why they are silent in this instance is that they have nodded off, damn them!

The Gregarious Bed

Although traditionally the double bed was designed for two, there are no rules and the gregariousness of double-bed life has always been part of its charm and a considerable part of its excitement.

Very many cases of fornication were between maidservants and either fellow-servants in the house or their masters. This temptation was greatly aggravated by the overcrowding in bedrooms, for the maid not infrequently slept in the same room as the master and mistress of the house. Some masters were frank about the services they expected, like the man who offered a girl '40s. to serve him by day and 40s. to lie with him on nights'.
(LAWRENCE STONE, *THE FAMILY, SEX AND MARRIAGE IN ENGLAND 1500–1800*)

THE CASE OF DELICACY

. . . I forthwith took possession of my bed-chamber – got a good fire – ordered supper; and was thanking heaven it was no worse – when a voiture arrived with a lady in it and her servant-maid.

As there was no other bed-chamber in the house, the hostess, without much nicety, led them into mine, telling them as she ushered them in, that there was nobody in it but an English gentleman – that there were two good beds in it, and a closet within the room which held another – the accent in which she spoke of this third bed did not say much for it – however, she said, there were three beds, and but three people – and she durst say, the gentleman would do anything to accommodate matters. I left not the lady a moment to make a conjecture about it – so instantly made a declaration I would do anything in my power.

As this did not amount to an absolute surrender of my bed-chamber, I still felt myself so much the proprietor as to have a right to do the honours of it – so I desired the lady to sit down – pressed her into the warmest seat – called for more wood – desired the hostess to enlarge the plan of the supper, and to favour us with the very best wine.

The lady had scarce warmed herself five minutes at the fire, before she began to turn her head back, and give a look at the beds; and the oftener she cast her eyes that way, the more they returned perplexed – I felt for her – and for myself; for in a few minutes, what by her looks, and the case itself, I found myself as much embarrassed as it was possible the lady could be herself.

That the beds we were to lie in were in one and the same room was enough simply by itself to have excited all this – but the position of them, for they stood parallel, and so very close to each other as only to allow space for a small wicker chair betwixt them, rendered the affair still more oppressive to us – they were fixed up moreover near the fire, and the projection of the chimney on one side, and a large beam which crossed the room on the other, formed a kind of recess for them that was in no way favourable to the nicety of our sensations – if anything could have added to it, it was, that the two beds were both of 'em so very small, as to cut us off from every idea of the lady and the maid lying together; which in either of them, could it have been feasible, my lying besides them, though a thing not to be wished, yet there was nothing in it so terrible which the imagination might not have passed over without torment.

We sat down to supper, and the lady, having a few bottles of Burgundy in her voiture, sent down her fille de chambre for a couple of them; so that by the time supper was over, and we were alone, we felt ourselves inspired with a strength of mind sufficient to talk at least without reserve upon our situation. We turned it every way, and debated and considered it in all kind of lights in the course of a two hours negotiation; at the end of which the articles were settled finally betwixt us, and stipulated for in form and manner of a treaty of peace.

They were as follows:

First. As the right of the bed-chamber is in Monsieur, and he thinking the bed next to the fire to be the warmest, he insists upon the concession on the lady's side of taking up with it.

Granted on the part of Madame; with a proviso, that as the curtains of that bed are of a flimsy transparent cotton, and appear likewise too scanty to draw close, that the fille de chambre shall fasten up the opening, either by corking pins or needle and thread, in such manner as shall be deemed a sufficient barrier on the side of Monsieur.

Secondly. It is required on the part of Madame, that Monsieur shall lay the whole night through in his robe de chambre.

Rejected: inasmuch as Monsieur is not worth a robe de chambre; he having nothing in his portmanteau but six shirts and a black silk pair of breeches.

The mentioning of the silk pair of breeches made an acceptive change of the article – for the breeches were accepted as an equivalent for the robe de chambre; and so it was stipulated and agreed upon that I should lie in my black silk breeches all night.

Thirdly. It was insisted upon, and stipulated for by the lady, that after Monsieur was got to bed, and the candle and fire extinguished, that Monsieur should not speak one single word the whole night.

Granted: provided Monsieur's saying his prayers might not be deemed an infraction of the treaty.

There was but one point forgot in this treaty, and that was the manner in which the lady and myself should be obliged to undress and get into bed – there was but one way of doing it, and that I leave to the reader to devise; protesting as I do it, that if it is not the most delicate in nature, 'tis the fault of his own imagination – against which this is not my first complaint.

Now when we were got to bed, whether it was the novelty of the situation, or what it was, I know not, but so it was I could not shut my eyes; I tried this side and that, and turned and turned again, till a full hour after midnight, when nature and patience both wearing out – O my God! said I –

– You have broke the treaty, Monsieur, said the lady, who had no more slept than myself. – I begged a thousand pardons – but insisted it was no more than an ejaculation – she maintained 'twas an entire infraction of the treaty – I maintained it was provided for in the clause of the third article.

The lady would by no means give up her point, though she weakened her barrier by it; for in the warmth of the dispute, I could hear two or three corking pins fall out of the curtain to the ground.

Upon my word and honour, Madame, said I – stretching my arm out of bed by way of asseveration –

– (I was going to have added, that I would not have trespassed against the remotest idea of decorum for the world) –

– But the fille de chambre hearing there were words between us, and fearing that hostilities would ensue in course, had crept silently out of her *closet, and it being totally dark, had stolen so close to our beds, that she had got herself into the narrow passage which separated them, and had advanced so far up as to be in a line betwixt her mistress and me –*

So that when I stretched out my hand, I caught hold of the fille de chambre's ——

E N D

(LAURENCE STERNE, *A SENTIMENTAL JOURNEY*)

Basil went into the dark little study next to the front door and rang up the Trumpingtons.

'Sonia, are you and Alastair doing anything tonight?'

'We're at home, Basil, what have you been doing to Alastair? I'm furious with you. I think he's going to die.'

'We had rather a racket. Shall I come to dinner?'

'Yes, do. We're in bed.'

He drove to Montagu Square and was shown up to their room. They lay in a vast, low bed, with a backgammon board between them. Each had a separate telephone, on the tables at the side, and by the telephone a goblet of 'black velvet'. A bull terrier and chow flirted on their feet. There were other people in the room: one playing the gramophone, one reading, one trying Sonia's face things at the dressing-table. Sonia said, 'It's such a waste not going out after dark. We have to stay in all day because of the duns.'

Alastair said, 'We can't have dinner with these infernal dogs all over the place.'

Sonia: 'You're a cheerful chap to be in bed with, aren't you?' and to the dog, 'Was oo called infernal woggie by owid man? Oh God, he's made a mess again.'

Alastair: 'Are those chaps staying to dinner?'

'We asked one.'

'Which?'

'Basil.'

'Don't mind him, but all those others.'

'I do hope not.'

They said, 'Afraid we'll have to. It's so late to go anywhere else.'

Basil: 'How dirty the bed is, Sonia.'

'I know. It's Alastair's dog. Anyway, you're a nice one to talk about dirt.'

'Isn't London hell?'

Alastair: 'I don't, anyway, see why those chaps shouldn't have dinner downstairs.'

They said: 'It would be more comfortable.'

'What are their names?'

'One we picked up last night. The other has been staying here for days.'

'It's not only the expense I mind. They're boring.'

They said: 'We wouldn't stay a moment if we had anywhere else to go.'

'Ring for dinner, sweet. I forget what there is, but I know it's rather good. I ordered it myself.'

There was whitebait, grilled kidneys and toasted cheese. Basil sat between them on the bed and they ate from their knees. Sonia threw a kidney to the dogs and they began a fight.

Alastair: 'It's no good. I can't eat anything.'

(EVELYN WAUGH, *BLACK MISCHIEF*)

No one in 1949 thought of objecting to <u>sisters</u> in bed together – not even the Hays Code. Today the same juxtaposition would probably need an X certificate: <u>Little Women</u>, Elizabeth Taylor and Margaret O'Brien

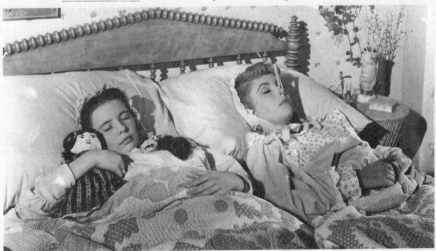

Precedents for Remaining in a Double Bed

Saw something in the woodshed and hasn't been the same since.
Aunt Ada Doom in *Cold Comfort Farm* (Stella Gibbons)

The only place in which to drink 'Black Velvet'.
Alastair and Sonia Digby-Vane-Trumpington in
Put Out More Flags (Evelyn Waugh)

The only place in which to have a baby.
Scarlett O'Hara in *Gone with the Wind* (Margaret Mitchell)

So deeply peaceful after the hurly-burly of the chaise longue.
Mrs Patrick Campbell

The only place in which to turn a spy into a double spy.
James Bond in *From Russia with Love* (Ian Fleming)

An unequalled location for the extraction of secrets.
Mata Hari

The respectable way to lose one's virginity.
Barbara Cartland

To give peace a chance.
John and Yoko Ono

To destroy the peace of others.
The Imaginary Invalid (Molière)

Insufficiency of clean linen to be seen walking in the street.
Baudelaire

Sloth.
Dr Johnson

The Working Bed

'My Office – My Sanctuary – My Bed'

CHRISTIAN DIOR

So far we have considered the double bed as a palace of pleasure, but there is no doubt that the real charm of double-bed life is that it can be the home of a fantasy of variety. From a double bed one can receive friends, compose poems and symphonies, create epigrams and works of art. Some of the most successful books of the best-selling author Jackie Collins have been written from the refuge of her bed, to which she retires after breakfast for the whole day with several exercise books, a multitude of pencils and a box of chocolates. Six months later, from the jumble of sheets and pillows and crumpled chocolate papers, emerges a five-hundred-page novel. Ms Collins is hardly alone in her preference for the sanctuary of her bed as a place of work. We know that Mark Twain was a great bed man, as was Voltaire who when he was sent in disgrace from the court of Versailles continued to write in glowing terms of his great friend Madame de Pompadour from the cosiness of his bed.

Winston Churchill was one of those rare creatures, a man who worked brilliantly from his double bed but seldom needed it for sleeping purposes. During the darkest hours of the Second World War he rarely slept for longer than an hour or so at a time and preferred to take 'cat-naps' to keep his wits about him. These, he always said, extracted the last ounce of energy from the human fabric. When it was all over and he could safely assume his side had won, he retired to his bed to dictate most of his *History of the Second World War*. His grandson and namesake, Winston S. Churchill M.P., remembers his grandfather in his later years holding court each morning from his bedroom at Chartwell. He would sit, propped up with a mass of cushions behind his head, a small bed table across his knees — cut out, apparently, to fit the shape of his belly — with his spectacles on the end of his nose, receiving family and friends. His table would hold a very weak whisky and soda and a somewhat damp cigar which would spend as much time dead as alight.

Milton apparently wrote *Paradise Lost* in bed. Shelley tried to write poetry from the same retreat but tended to lose his pencils. Wordsworth, however, was extremely adept at writing not only in bed, but in total darkness too. (This news should silence once and for all those detractors who maintain that William stole most of his ideas from his sister Dorothy's diary. He couldn't see his own writing, let alone hers.)

Elinor Glyn, who has more to do with double beds than most, was another who found her bed more than a place of sexual pleasure. In order to pay a £1,000 debt for her husband she impetuously agreed to write a 90,000-word novel in the space of three weeks. It was a tour de force. Propped up in bed and fortified with quantities of coffee and brandy, she wrote day and night and actually beat her deadline by three days.

Not all writers restricted their bedtime creativity to literature. G. K. Chesterton was fascinated by the idea of painting his bedroom ceiling while lying in bed. It would involve, he decided, a long broom and a selection of different coloured paints in pails beside the bed. The result would undoubtedly have been bizarre and original but the side effects might have been less agreeable. The paint, he pondered, 'might drip down again on one's face in floods of rich and mingled colour like some strange fairy rain'. (This was a distinct possibility and it is easy to see why Chesterton decided against mural painting on the ceiling – at least for himself.) He was a puritan as far as any other bedtime indulgence was concerned, however, maintaining that anyone lying in bed who was not severely ill, was little more than a layabout and probably a hypochondriac to boot.

He might, however, have approved of the French artist Henri Matisse, who attempted something similar to Chesterton's artistic antics when he became bedridden in old age. Matisse tied one of his charcoals to a long stick and continued to practise his art in black and white on his bedroom walls. It is strange that fragments of these walls have not appeared for sale at enormous cost on the art market. If a Lautrec menu fetches a million francs, what price a Matisse wall?

For many artists the bed was a favoured place of work simply because it was the one place where they could keep warm. A well-known fact of artistic life is that most artists have to die before they become outrageously successful (with a few notable exceptions busily proving the rule) and so many of them sat huddled in their bedclothes spilling the paint water in the sheets and losing the brushes in their mattresses, creating works of art that have since sold for thousands. Fantin Latour often worked in bed because he could not afford a fire. During the winter when not even his bedclothes offered enough warmth he used to add a thin coat, a scarf and his top hat. Thus protected from the bitter cold he would sketch for hours with only a candle to light his way.

Other great artists have found the bed a source of inspiration if not the best place to work: Toulouse Lautrec, Rembrandt for his 'Danae', Van

Gogh, Goya for 'The Naked Maya', Delacroix for his 'Nude with White Stockings' and hosts of others. The bed, and, it must be admitted, its nude occupants, have fascinated artists since the first pictures were scratched on to the first cave walls.

My favourite story of the artist in bed concerns the Italian opera composer Rossini. He was a great bed man, scribbling away at his crotchets and quavers from under the sheets and rarely, if ever, allowing his feet to touch the floor. Once, when he had just completed an aria it fluttered off the bed out of reach. He was so comfortable and so loath to move that he could not be bothered to climb out to retrieve it, and so he promptly wrote another. Such laziness! Such talent! Such style!

Even ordinary bed activities like reading can be fraught with peril. For years schoolchildren have played havoc with their eyesight as they pore over forbidden literature under the bedclothes with no better light than a torch. Before the days of electricity the dangers were even worse. Baron Puckler-Muskaue wrote in 1828: 'The bad habit of reading in bed occasioned me a laughable misfortune last night. My hair caught fire.'

Luckily the chances of one's hair catching fire while reading even the steamiest novel are fairly rare in these modern times. Creative bedtime life is much easier to achieve with the proximity of the telephone and, for the extremely lucky, room service. The American eccentric, Howard Hughes, is said to have spent the last few years of his life in bed. When he did deign to walk a few steps, he insisted on wearing sterile tissue boxes on his feet to keep out the germs. A more recent American eccentric, Hugh Hefner, incorporated several features in his famous round bed in order to make his working life less of a hassle. His bed, which could rotate through 360 degrees, was designed so that if he needed a pencil that happened to be on the wrong side of the bed he could simply turn it around like a gramophone turntable.

There are less eccentric people, whose beds are not of the custom-made variety, who still enjoy the indulgence of a working life in bed. One London publicist maintains that he leaves his only in a real emergency, such as a client's first night or a book publisher's party. The best kind of bed, he says, is the one that never gets made, but is just hoovered occasionally.

Barbara Cartland – whose bed is an inspiration

Publicists, more than any other breed, would happily bring back the use of the *lit de parade* or state bed. This hugely popular custom was begun in Renaissance times and lasted until the French Revolution. The rich, the powerful and the fashionable entertained and received visitors from the comfort of their beds. Naturally women, particularly pretty ones, were amongst the first to take to the fashion, arranging themselves *en déshabille*, wearing the sexiest and most seductive garments.

The trend began, naturally enough, when ladies of quality took to their beds when they were pregnant. There they would prettily accept the felicitations of their visitors. The fashion then extended to the mourning of a husband or beloved relative. This perfectly reasonable expression of great loss and bereavement soon became a social ritual, requiring a properly respectable period of 'lying in'. In his memoirs the Marshal de Flearanges wrote of the death of Louis XIII: 'It is the custom with the Queens of France that when the King is dead they remain six weeks in bed.'

Another charming custom was one affected by young brides, who received visitors in bed on the day after the wedding, presumably to advertise the virility of the new husbands. So great was their ardour supposed to be, and so demanding were they of their new and innocent brides, that the breathless young wives could barely rise from their beds after such a strenuous event. But it was not only the erstwhile maidens who were allowed the sybaritic pleasure of *lits de parades*. Quite often mothers, aunts and sisters would do the same, retiring to their beds on the marriage of a daughter, niece or sister in order to receive congratulations from their many visitors. Two of Louis XIV's mistresses gracefully took to their beds on the marriage announcements of favourite nieces. In a letter to Madame de Sévigné in 1695, Mademoiselle de Coularges wrote of how Madame de Montespan married off Mademoiselle de Thianges and then went to bed to receive the compliments of the French court. Her successor, Madame de Maintenon, did the same several years later when she married Mademoiselle d'Aubigné to the Comte d'Ayen.

Once this fashion was established excuses became superfluous, and ladies of rank would scurry off to bed at the slightest opportunity. When a certain Mademoiselle de Fontages was created a duchess with an income of twenty thousand crowns a year, she retired to bed to receive the congratulations of the king and his courtiers. In this instance, it has to be admitted, her bed was the appropriate place in which to receive her reward for services rendered.

It must have been highly enjoyable to accept one's friends' congratulations on anything from the engagement of a fifth niece twice removed to the engagement of one's best friend's favourite cook from the comfort of a bed. There was the added advantage that ladies could entertain male visitors in a perfectly respectable but highly suggestive fashion. Unfortunately, the custom was expensive and husbands began to rebel against paying for an extravagance they were the last to enjoy, as wives vied with each other in flaunting the most luxurious, most extravagant bedroom finery. Mercifully the stern hand of the law made itself felt throughout most European countries in the eighteenth century, when silk counterpanes or those embroidered with gold or silver were outlawed. Silk chemises were also not allowed. Such a petty move, because anyone who knows anything about the charm of double beds, knows that such charm is dependent, not on the grandness of the dressing, but on the quality of the undressing.

Actress Clair Martin on her mobile bed with a headboard reminiscent of a car dashboard, plus stereo, spotlights, wrap-around mirror and finished in beige suedette: JODY BOULTING

Much later, speaking from her own version of the *lit de parade*, Marilyn Monroe, on being asked what she had on when she went to bed, answered 'the radio', and when pressed as to what she *wore* replied: 'Chanel No. 5.' She was not the only film star to attempt to bring back the *lit de parade*. Jayne Mansfield, who achieved fame in the 1950s because of her forty-two-inch bosom, had a pink heart-shaped bed in which she was photographed at every available opportunity. Men are also susceptible to the conceits of the *lit de parade*. Christian Dior, doyen of French couture, used to hold court from his bed, sketching designs and discussing ideas.

The wonderful thing about the double bed as a platform from which to air opinions, is that somehow the very softness of its appearance adds substance to what is being said. An epigram delivered from bed assumes a spontaneous quality. How witty, how amusing to think of the *bon mot* just like that – *in bed* – as if thinking of something in bed is much cleverer than thinking of something in an office or behind a desk. In fact, it is much easier to be brilliant from bed than from anywhere else. The bedtime philosopher does not have the distractions of what to wear, how to travel, or which route to take to avoid the traffic, but can concentrate on the observations. No wonder they emerge as wise and informed.

It is much easier to be tough, even ruthless, from bed. The comfortable surroundings detract from harsh reality. I knew a business tycoon who made it a habit to sack his employees from his bed. They would be invited to his version of the *lit de parade*, given coffee, offered orange juice and dismissed then and there. Perhaps his bed was not so much a *lit de parade* as a *lit de justice*, a much earlier sort of bed, from which a king or some other highly placed individual would pronounce judgement.

The *lit de justice* really came into its own in the fourteenth century, although Alexander the Great used to do business reclining on a bed of gold in the middle of an enormous tent, and the Romans used not only to eat and drink from their couches but also to give the thumbs up or down, depending on their mood, from the same position. It was in France, however, that the *lit de justice* was perfected. Whenever the king attended parliament he reclined not on a throne but a bed surrounded by his princes, who were seated, his chief officers of state, who stood, and lowly officials who respectfully knelt. The custom lasted in France until the fall of the monarchy. In his *Ceremonial*, François Godefroy describes the bed of justice held in 1527 by François I:

On the 24th July in the morning the King was on his royal seat and throne holding his Bed of Justice. Seven steps led up to the Bed covered in tapestry of blue velvet, sewn with golden fleurs de lys in the form of embroidery and over and above was a similar canopy. And round about, behind the said Lord the King and beneath his feet there were four large squares of the same material; and on the right side of the King, on the high seats of the bar, was the King of Navarre together with the others; on the left side, on the high seats was the Cardinal de Bourbon with others; at the feet of the King was the Duc de Longueville, Grand Chamberlain of France, the nearest to the King on the right side, lying on the highest step. In front of the King, kneeling were Anne de Resne, called Michelet, captain of Pont-de-See and the Sieur Nagu, ushers of the King's chamber, each holding his staff of office in his hand.

Two hundred years later Louis XV, whose sense of justice was eccentric, prompted the wit Fontenelle, when asked, 'What Sir, is a Bed of Justice?' to remark, 'It is the Place where Justice lies asleep.'

Portable interior spring mattress (1871)

Without doubt the greatest bed lover history has seen was His Eminence the Cardinal de Richelieu, scheming and brilliant minister of the Sun King, Louis XIV. During the last years of his life, the cardinal never left his bed at all, and actually travelled in it. His favourite bed was vast and of magnificent proportions. It was so big that in order to make room for it on his long journeys up and down France, it was often necessary to break down ramparts and gates of towns, and even walls and windows of houses. Modern conservationists who lobby against the destruction of homes and villages in order to accommodate motorways and road-widening schemes would sympathize with people of the time, who had little choice but to stand by helplessly as the preposterous cardinal travelled through. One of his contemporaries wrote of one such journey:

> Six powerful men carried the bed on two strong beams or bars and the places on which they had to put their hands were padded and strengthened with straps . . . Thus did these men carry the bed, and within it the said Lord, into the towns and into the houses where he was to lodge. What particularly astonished the populace was the fact that he entered into the houses through the windows; for before he arrived the masons whom he brought with him would break open the window casements of the houses, or would effect breaches in the walls of the rooms which he was to occupy and after that they would erect a wooden bridge between the street and the windows or the openings made in the walls of the house. Thus esconced in his portable bed, the Lord Cardinal passed through the streets and was transported over the bridge into the room in which another bed had been prepared and which his attendants had adorned with scarlet and violet damask and the richest possible furnishings.

(J. BANNE, *PASSAGE DU CARDINAL DE RICHELIEU À VIVIERS*)

No statesman could emulate Richelieu today, but modern ladies of the night continue to use their double beds as they always have, but with far less panache than their predecessors. What would the great courtesans make of today's call girls who answer a 'bleep' like district nurses and go from hotel bed to hotel bed scarcely noticing the client let alone the decoration? Such behaviour would never have done for such remarkable beings as the glorious La Païva who moved into the upper echelons of

French society in 1841. She was a sensational creature, quite plain with, it is said, slightly protruding eyes and a Mongolian nose. But she had lashings of style and during her eventful life she amassed an incredible fortune, demanding and getting unprecedented sums for her favours. One would-be lover, a certain Adolphe Gaiffe, requested the pleasure of her so often that she finally said: 'Bring me ten thousand francs in notes and we'll set light to them, and I will be yours as long as they are burning.' Monsieur Gaiffe was not a rich man, but he arrived the next day, with twelve thousand, or so the story goes. The Grande Horizontale was true to her word and entertained him until the last note was reduced to ashes. It was only then that he told her that the pile of precious bank notes had been forged. She would never again display such a cavalier attitude towards money.

La Païva was renowned throughout Paris thereafter for her respect for every franc that came her way. But to be fair to her it must be said that she did plough her assets back into her business. Her '*hôtel*', as her house in Paris was called, was the talk of the town, particularly the bedroom, which was reached via a staircase made entirely of onyx and carved with the legend, 'Vice, like virtue, has its steps.' The *pièce de résistance* was her double bed, which triumphantly displayed the art of the true courtesan. It was encrusted with rare woods and ivory, and on the ceiling above, the Goddess Aurora hovered enticingly. The cost was phenomenal: one hundred thousand gold francs. The original estimate was for fifty thousand but when this figure was quoted, the lady cried: 'Fifty thousand francs? You want me to have fleas? Make it one hundred thousand.'

Like other great parvenues of her time, La Païva gave sparkling and munificent parties where the rich and powerful mixed with the fashionable and artistic. One of her favourite guests was the critic and journalist Théophile Gautier, whose great friendship with another brilliant courtesan of the time, Alice Ozy, did not stop him from partaking of the fruits of her rival's table. It is unlikely that Gautier enjoyed much more than food and drink from La Païva, but he was a lover of the classically beautiful Alice for many years and enjoyed her favours in her less ostentatious but still lavishly designed rosewood bed. This was decorated with Sèvres medallions of cupids, and draped in fragile, delicate swathes of lace. But her most valued lover and the man she seems to have truly cared for, was the artist Theodore Chasseriau who painted this dazzling creature reclining in her bed. The picture is dated 1850 when Alice Ozy was thirty years old, quite ancient by the standards of the day, but she still maintained a suggestion of the innocence and naïveté that had captivated her lovers from the beginning of her career, when she was thirteen.

The profession shared by La Païva and Alice Ozy along with so many others may be considered the oldest in the world, but in nineteenth-century France it could also be distinguished. The French have always treated the bed with great respect; nobles and courtiers in the seventeenth and eighteenth centuries would even genuflect or curtsey while in the presence of the hallowed royal bed. It is not surprising, therefore, that the cult of the bed (as a kind of barometer of culture) reached its height in Europe and, in particular, in France. The reverence with which it was treated does not exist today, but we are still left with a vague sense of the power of the bed. It is possibly this subconscious awareness that makes it the subject of our worst dreams and most frightening fears.

Every child has experienced the stark terror of the absolute certainty that there are wolves, lions or tigers hiding under the bed. I know of a

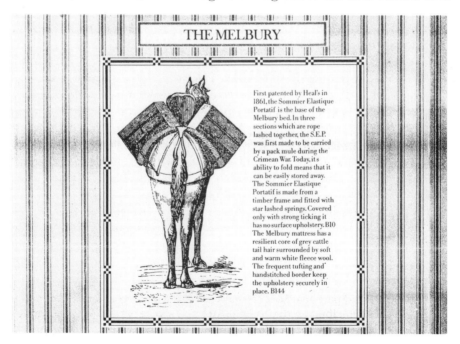

THE MELBURY

First patented by Heal's in 1861, the Sommier Elastique Portatif is the base of the Melbury bed. In three sections which are rope lashed together, the S.E.P. was first made to be carried by a pack mule during the Crimean War. Today, its ability to fold means that it can be easily stored away. The Sommier Elastique Portatif is made from a timber frame and fitted with star lashed springs. Covered only with strong ticking it has no surface upholstery. B10 The Melbury mattress has a resilient core of grey cattle tail hair surrounded by soft and warm white fleece wool. The frequent tufting and handstitched border keep the upholstery securely in place. B144 nanny who used systematically to roll a broom handle along the bed from head to foot to get rid of robbers or bogey men. Most of these robbers or bogey men were strictly imaginary, but in 1850 'boy Jones', an intruder into Buckingham Palace, was found in the palace nursery. He was harmless and did little more than skulk about experiencing the heady joys of palace life while everyone else slept. One hundred and thirty years later another palace intruder, Michael Fagin, did much the same thing. He managed to sneak into Buckingham Palace and found the queen in her nightdress. He too was a harmless, somewhat unstable fellow but there was an enormous hue and cry about palace security. The excitement aroused was not only concern for the queen's safety, but also a symptom of the very human fascination over what sort of bed she slept in and what she wore. HM Queen Elizabeth, unlike most of her married subjects, sleeps in a single bed. What she wears is still unknown. Michael Fagin, in a rare moment of discretion, did not say.

No doubt it was a pretty harrowing experience for the queen and one that does not bear repeating but it was not as extraordinary as this anecdote, which was catalogued by the redoubtable Augustus Hare in *The Story of My Life* (1896–1900). He was writing at the time about a lady of his acquaintance who was:

> *awoken in the night with the disagreeable sense of not being alone in the room and soon felt a thud upon her bed. There was no doubt that someone was moving to and fro in the room and that hands were constantly moving over her bed. She was so dreadfully frightened that at last she fainted. When she came to herself it was broad daylight and she found that the butler had walked in his sleep and had laid the table for fourteen upon her bed.*

How satisfying to find that life continues to imitate art and that in the tradition of the best stage thriller the butler did it – again.

The Melbury. First patented by Heal's in 1861, the Sommier Elastique Portatif is the base of the Melbury bed. This was first made to be carried by a pack mule during the Crimean War: HEAL & SON

UNDERCOVER STORY

Georges Mikes once wrote that 'on the continent they have sex, in England they have hot water bottles', but in a later book revealed that he had been soundly reprimanded on this observation and accused of being old-fashioned, out of date and wrong. 'These days,' he was told, 'we have electric blankets.'

Such stories give electric blankets and hot water bottles a bad name. Both are wonderful and have their own very special part to play in double-bed comfort. They should never however be treated as a substitute. Not even a sexual one.

A well-dressed double bed should boast an extensive wardrobe and should be able to cater for all occasions.

Opposite: top
This could be the outright winner in 'the most uncomfortable bed' competition (third bird cage is optional): bedroom designed and carried out by Fortnum & Mason Ltd, London during the 1930s. CoID PHOTOGRAPH

Opposite: bottom
Bedroom designed and carried out by Fortnum & Mason Ltd, London, during the 1930s: CoID PHOTOGRAPH

An exhaustive supply of crisply pressed sheets, fitted and otherwise and mostly plain white. All sheets to be ironed all the way down and not just on the turnups.

Twice the amount of pillow cases to take care of numerous pillows.

One set of satin sheets for epic seduction scenes. If you have a sense of humour and can face them in the morning go for black but most sensitive souls plump for ivory or white. (Do practise on your own first. Satin sheets are so slippery they demand a special technique if the whole episode is not going to dissolve into high farce.)

A duvet filled with high-quality terylene (goosedown is all very well but what about possible allergic bed partners).

A selection of woolly blankets for duvet haters.

Two hot water bottles in furry covers (not real fur).

One electric underblanket with controls at both sides of the bed.

Two thick, towelling robes, the biggest you can buy. (All women feel more attractive in a robe that's too big for them and all men feel flattered that you thought they were that size.)

Double Beds for Old-Timers – and Gourmets

'I am happy now that Charles calls on my bedchamber less frequently than of old. As it is now I endure but two calls a week and when I hear his steps outside my door I lie down on my bed, close my eyes, open my legs and think of England.'

LADY HILLINGDON, JOURNAL 1912

LADY HILLINGDON'S RESIGNED attitude towards sex was considered only right and proper for an older woman in 1912. Even today sex is still considered a sport for those under fifty. In fact, nothing could be further from the truth. The glint in the eye of a seventy-year-old bridegroom can be equalled only by the twinkle in the eye of his sixty-year-old bride. Both of them can be just as wanton, just as enthusiastic (if a trifle more careful) than lovers half their age.

History tells, for example, of one Thomas Parr, who was born in the English county of Shropshire in 1483 and was said to have remarried at the age of 120. His fifty-two-year-old bride was reported to have 'never noticed her husband's great age so well had he performed his conjugal duties'. Thomas eventually died in 1635 aged 152.

There is a widely held belief that the pleasures of the double bed are merely physical. Indeed, amongst very young males, a double bed is seen more as a sports stadium than anything else, demanding an intensive training programme, a proper diet and regular exercise. Frequent practice is also encouraged at every available opportunity. You can spot sexual sportspersons any morning of the week, panting and sweating their way across parks and by-ways with the other joggers, getting themselves into condition for the night's activity. They are the ones who would never forgive themselves if they didn't 'do it' at least twice a night and feel like 'doing it' again at least once. Unfortunately, as with a great many sportspersons, those in the sexual arena are inclined to lose their perspective, not to mention their sense of humour and get hung up on breaking records – not world records, but those established by their best friends, their drinking chums or their wives' brothers. The categories in their sport are not complicated and are unhindered by rules. There are only three.

1) How often?
2) How many?
3) For how long?

Sexual athletes are hardly a twentieth-century invention. Augustin Cabanes, in *An Illustrated Treasury of Scientific Marvels of Human Sexuality* published in 1933, wrote of a former Duc d'Orléans who in the eighteenth century wished to inform the world that he had made love to a certain Mademoiselle Deschamps twelve times in one night. So that there would be no mistaking that magic figure, Cabanes wrote:

. . . he had the number twelve imprinted on the buttons of his breeches, coats and hats. He had his shirts marked with the figure twelve. He wanted to have everything in dozens: twelve guns, twelve swords, twelve settings for his table, twelve dishes on his menu. Each day his treasurer delivered to him twelve hundred francs for pocket money and when he bestowed a little tip or a present it was twelve francs or twelve louis.

Another of Cabanes' heroes was Charles V of France, who never performed less than three times in a night. 'When he slept with a fair lady, (for he was fond of loving – too much so for his gout), he never went away without thrice having had his pleasure of her.'

Obviously those hooked on sex as a sport find the very idea of a couple of old-timers enjoying the sensual pleasure of a good snuggle and whatever else may occur both disturbing and inconceivable. Yet of all those who enjoy double-bed life no other category has the same opportunity to enjoy it to the full. Old-timers alone can stay in bed all day and all night if they want to. Unless hobbies, charity work and minding the grandchildren absorb every waking hour, some old-timers can truthfully claim they have nothing else to do. Not for them the office, the commuter special, the daily pressures of working life. Bed can take over. One couple of old-timers I knew found that by making their bed their hobby they had, after thirty-seven years of marriage, at last discovered an interest they could share. He could never stand bridge and she had loathed golf for most of their married life, but in his retirement their bed and the life they shared in it became a joint passion. It began with breakfast, which they scrupulously took turns to prepare, each competing with the other to discover the ideal breakfast in bed. Toast was out – too many crumbs – bacon always smelt better than it tasted and eggs were too unimaginative. Bracing British breakfasts featuring kippers or slivers of liver are easy enough to eat in bed but leave unappetizing odours behind them. Mushrooms look nasty if spilled and are inclined to smell like lion's cages, while bowls of breakfast cereal are just asking for trouble. All that snap, crackle and pop is noisy and irritating. American breakfasts of waffles or pancakes are just right for bedtime enjoyment, but unless proper equipment is supplied in the form of bed tables with firm unshakable trays, essentials like the jug of maple syrup play havoc with the mattress.

Bedtime eating does not have to be confined to breakfast. After all, the ancient Greeks used to enjoy all their meals in bed *except* breakfast. Luncheon, their equivalent of afternoon tea, and supper were each taken in the reclining position and there is no reason in the world why old-timers, or indeed any timers at all who have the time and inclination, should not adopt their customs.

The trick lies in finding the right food for the moment. The traditional hearty meal of roast beef or steak and kidney pudding that is supposed to lull a man into a sense of wellbeing and deep satisfaction is ideal at table but all wrong in bed. Any food or drink that is heavy, awkward to handle or requires too much concentration is not suitable bedtime eating. Luxurious food in smallish quantities is perfect. Two bowls full of strawberries and cream with iced champagne would be ideal in summer. A few quails' eggs with a little caviar and soft toast might be even better in that they combine lightness, luxury and the legendary aphrodisiac qualities of the eggs.

Some famous lovers have sworn by cheese as the food of love. Casanova, who spent almost as much time concocting suitable menus as he did actually seducing women, was a great believer in the persuasive charms of soft French cheeses such as Roquefort. Those who decide to follow his example should do so with caution. Roquefort is all very well, as would be chèvre, Brie or Camembert, but do not be tempted to substitute Cheddar or Double Gloucester if the soft cheeses are not available. Not only do they crumble and rub into the sheets in an unpleasant way but they are fiercely indigestible to some, and a bedtime partner with a stomach ache is worse than no bedtime partner at all.

For anyone who has the time there is no better style of bedtime eating than that perfected by the experts: the chefs, probably eunuchs poor things, who concocted all manner of delicious bits and pieces in the Turkish harems. Imagine a dish called 'And the Imam fainted', so named because the priest who thought he was to be denied such a gourmet delight promptly fainted with horror. It features the soft, beguiling eggplant with lots of tomatoes and herbs like basil and oregano. It does take considerable time to prepare but if double-bed life could be seen as a one day on, one day off affair with the day off used for preparing the menus for the day on then the chances of boredom setting in become more remote.

The great charm of eating in the Middle Eastern fashion is that the dishes are shared. There is no need for food to be divided on to separate plates. Instead the Arabic and Turkish way is to provide big dishes filled with succulent food from which everyone eats. Knives and forks are superfluous at such a meal; fingers and flat, unleavened Arabic bread are all that is required. The bread should be slightly toasted so that when it is ripped open the warm doughy steam inside sets the taste buds in motion and produces a seductive atmosphere all of its own. After such a meal the Turks used to produce sweetmeats filled with warm honey and nuts, with names like 'Lovers' Lips' and 'Ladies' Navels', and these were eaten with tiny cups of thick Turkish coffee and an array of voluptuous fruits, such as figs with their bright pink flesh, or melons and persimmons and peeled black grapes dipped in sugar.

Not all old-timers will wish to go quite this far but if double-bed life is to become an addictive hobby then it is as well to arrange it properly. In the absence of fingerbowls, which are just asking for trouble, a Turkish or Arabic feast should be concluded in the Eastern style with hot, scented towels to cleanse the fingers and cool the brow. Traditionally, such a meal would be served without alcohol because according to the Koran Moslems must not drink, which perhaps helps to explain how the Sultan could still, after eating his fill, drop his royal handkerchief in front of the lady who most pleased him and then proceed to please her by making love all night.

Shakespeare once remarked that drink provokes the desire but takes away the performance, which many would-be lovers have proved to their cost. A great many men still believe that if you give a girl enough to drink she will tip over and lie down. She does, but usually because she has passed out. The effect on a man is even worse. He may be amorous but he has been rendered impotent. Rabelais understood this well when he pointed out, 'that is why Bacchus, god of drunkards, is painted beardless and clad in women's clothes, an effeminate and ballock-less eunuch'.

It is obviously wise to be very careful when choosing any liquor to accompany double-bed eating. Champagne is ideal. Naturally it should be good champagne and taken in moderate quantities. The very best way of buying champagne for double-bed consumption is in splits (quarter bottles) that stay colder longer and do not sit there half-emptied demanding to be finished before the fizz has gone. If this seems unnecessarily extravagant almost any dry white wine that can be bought in half bottles will suit double-bed life. Price is no guide here: a fresh young garden wine that does not cost very much can be wonderful in bed. It is still light, slightly fruity and is an accompaniment to the meal not the main event. Red wines have a sexier reputation and although heavier can be smooth and velvety – a seduction in themselves. Mouton Cadet is hard to beat, as are many of the Californian and Australian clarets that seem to have captured all the sunshine of their particular hillside, and can brighten up a European or North American winter in the most remarkable way. Having gone to all the trouble of finding the right wine it would be a pity to ruin the effect by serving it at the wrong temperature. Most red

The modern double bed with everything – even, if the picture is to be believed, its own shower: The 'House of the Future' designed by Alison and Peter Smithson for the 'Daily Mail Ideal Home Exhibition,' 1956. CoID COLLECTION

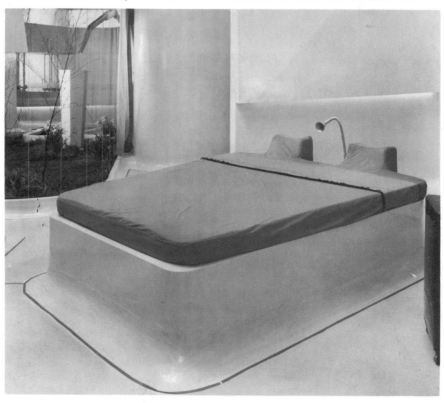

wines should be opened for at least an hour first and brought to room temperature, while white wine should be chilled and served in glasses that have been kept in the fridge. If double-bed eating is to become a way of life then a selection of the right glasses should be kept in the bedroom along with comfortable pillows and a stereo. However it should be pointed out that rules are made to be broken and an abandoned moment that features newly opened red wine drunk out of tooth glasses, accompanied by greasy fish and chips from around the corner, can be absolutely marvellous.

Naturally, committed old-timers who are intent on making their double-bed life a sparkling, witty affair invest in the right sort of equipment from the very beginning. As always, style is everything and plastic bedtime trays with collapsible legs have no part to play in sexy, charming double-bed life. They are ideal for invalids and those unfortunate enough to be stuck in hospital, but they are not for anyone whose concern is sybaritic enjoyment. My old-timer friends were the first to find those trays with gently cushioned undersides that are perfect for breakfast, luncheon or an intimate dinner in bed. The trays squelch down on the knees in a satisfying way and have no hospital overtones. What is more, once their official purpose has been served they can be gently pushed away just like any other pillows, and there is no danger of their legs sticking into anyone else's and destroying a mood.

There is yet another delight unique to old-timers. Unlike almost everyone else they are highly unlikely to be disturbed. No matter how loving, affectionate or caring children may be, nothing makes them feel better than the thought that their parents do not have to be visited every five minutes. So instead of sulking over the fact that apart from Sundays and Bank Holidays they might as well not exist, old-timers should take advantage of what can be seen as visit-free days; days when the two of them can simply enjoy each other.

At this stage adventurous old-timers might do well to consider the aphrodisiac. The egg, in any form, is purported to have aphrodisiac properties and the oyster is famous for its amorous image but what else? Research leads me to believe that almost everything edible has at some time been claimed to have miracle properties. The *Kama Sutra* advises the drinking of milk mixed with sugar, the root of the uchchata, the piber chaba and licorice for a man who wishes to have his sexual vigour restored. It also maintains that 'if a man mixes rice with the eggs of the sparrow and having boiled this in milk, adds to it ghee and honey and drinks as much of it as necessary he will be able to enjoy innumerable women'.

This kind of advice can be very disheartening for the modern lover who has little chance of finding any uchchata root or a scrap of piber chaba, but Sir Richard Burton, whose interest in the erotic horrified his fellow Victorians, maintained that although rhinoceros horn was renowned for its aphrodisiac effect, peas, beans, artichokes, lettuce, radishes, leeks, almonds, pine nuts, snails, mussels, fruit, etc. were all excellent foods for stimulating sexual activity. Earlier scribes maintained that not only shellfish but all fish have an aphrodisiac effect. So have garlic and onions but it is wise to chew plenty of parsley after eating them.

Aphrodisiacs must not be confused with love potions, which were used for an entirely different purpose. All sorts of people who should have known better were said to pay highly for a 'magic philtre' when their love was unrequited. The clever and sophisticated Madame de Montespan paid fifty crowns for hers. Philtres contained unmentionable nasties, including essence of bats' wing and liver of toad, but others sound really rather nice. In her introduction to *Food for Lovers* Pamela Michael describes an old recipe based on myrtle water, said to have been used by the Goddess Venus 'in her most intimate toilet'.

The flowers and leaves of myrtle, two handfuls, infuse them in two quarts of spring water and a quart of white wine, twenty-four hours and then distil them in a cold still and this will be of strong scent and tincture and by adding more or less myrtle you may make it stronger or weaker as you please.

A lover who sipped this philtre mixed with cordial syrup not only had a delicious drink but was inclined, so it was believed, to become wondrously amorous.

While it is tempting to try such a delightful recipe, it is as well to remember that most foods are said to act as a sexual stimulant, and if you have not noticed any particular effect yourself over the years, the chances of success at this stage are pretty slim. One early cynic, Norman Douglas, wrote: 'Put not your trust in Arabian skink, in Roman goose-fat or Roman goose tongues, in the arplan of China that "maketh a man renew his youth and astonish his household".' None of them will make a blind bit of difference according to Douglas. He listed as many foods as he could think of, and concluded: 'Aphrodisiacs all, and all imposters.'

Happily energy and enthusiasm in so-called old age are not dependent on mixtures, potions or any form of aphrodisiac. Jeremiah Hobson and his wife retired to their double bed as soon as he had received his gold watch for faithful service with the Canadian Pacific Railways. A hard-working and God-fearing couple they had never thought of sensual pleasure in their entire married life, but once the pressures of children and job were lifted from his shoulders, Jeremiah Hobson became a different man. He read *The Perfumed Garden* from cover to cover and could not wait to get on to the *Kama Sutra*. 'He'd never thought about reading before,' his wife remarked thoughtfully, 'and now he can't get enough of it.' Quite so.

As Aunt Augusta, Graham Greene's delightful heroine of *Travels with My Aunt* pointed out to her dull, ex-bank manager nephew: 'Age, Henry, may a little modify our emotions. It doesn't destroy them.' Few writers have understood the vagaries of human passion as well as Graham Greene. In the same story he wraps up neatly and perfectly the joy and wonderfully selfish pleasure of unquestioning love that has no age limit: 'When I entered the sala there remained only one couple – my aunt and Mr Visconti. They were dancing a slow waltz now and they never saw me enter, two old people bound in the deep incurable egotism of passion.'

When such old-timers retire to their beds for the fun of it, the choice of double bed is just as important as it was back in the heady days of youth. The bed that Jack built to consummate the marriage, to have the babies, to grow into children is not always the ideal bed in which to rediscover forgotten pleasures or to investigate new ones. Quirks that took years to identify and even longer to accept can now be catered for. Backs that need more support or less, pillows that need to be plumped up or flattened down or discarded completely, can all be taken into consideration.

It is most reassuring to find that manufacturers are beginning to see that the bedroom is another 'living' room and not just a place for sex, procreation or sleep. Bedside tables with cunningly hidden sliding trays for reading or eating or playing word games are starting to appear in furniture showrooms. Innovative ideas include 'Pillowsleep', a kind of cushioned stereo/radio manufactured by a team of clever insomniacs in the south of England. Hidden in the softest of pillows is a tiny amplifier, so that one can drift off to sleep lulled by a favourite piece of music. It is a brilliant idea and I defy even the princess who detected the pea under her multitude of mattresses to feel the physical presence of the electronic gadgetry.

According to my research the ideal bedroom for old-timers features a wide double bed with a matching double set of power points on each side. These are to cater for the bedside lamps, the automatic tea- or coffee-maker, the television set, the music centre and the electric blanket. A small fridge is vital in a well-equipped double-bed room, not just for the iced drinks, the ice-cream for dessert or the chilled champagne, but also for salted peanuts; kept in the fridge they leave fingers, and consequently sheets, less greasy. Naturally there is space for an assortment of reading matter, plenty of pens and paper and a pile of board games.

A well-equipped bedroom wardrobe is not jam-packed with clothes for the great outdoors but contains beguiling negligées, comfortable pyjamas and perfect dressing gowns. Marilyn Monroe may have slept with nothing on except the radio, but after a certain age such indulgences are just that, very indulgent. No old-timer wants to be like the lady in the joke who inspired two of her male contemporaries to remark as she walked naked through the turkish bath: 'The face is familiar old chap — but doesn't the dress need ironing?'

Double-Bed Fare

HERE IS A small selection of recipes for bedtime consumption. None is specifically for breakfast, luncheon, tea or supper. Double-bed life knows no such restrictions. Obviously each recipe is for two people.

Caviare and Sour Cream Omelette

4 large eggs
a dash of cold water
pepper and salt
a large knob of butter
a tiny tin of caviare or (if you must) pink or black lumpfish roe
4 teaspoons sour cream
a little chopped dill or parsley

Make each omelette separately, preferably in a proper omelette pan. Beat the eggs lightly with the water and seasoning. Melt the butter, and, making sure the pan is really hot, pour in the mixture. Let the eggs swirl around the pan so that the edges are cooked and the middle satisfyingly wet. Roll the omelette on to a heated plate, folding it over, and keep hot while you make the second one. When both are ready, slit them open and pile up with equal shares of caviare, topped with two teaspoons of sour cream. Sprinkle with dill or parsley and serve with white wine. (Champagne with caviare looks pretentious.)

(A cheese, ham, bacon or chicken omelette can be made in the same way, although the sour cream should be omitted, and the filling added during cooking. If the omelette is more mundane then the wine can be more special. Use your own judgement.)

M'tabl (Eggplant Purée)

1 large eggplant
2 tablespoons lemon juice
1 large clove garlic
half cup sesame paste (tahina, available in Greek and Lebanese
shops)
chopped parsley
olive oil

Grill or bake the eggplant until it is soft. If it is grilled, the skin should be charcoaled and the flesh like pulp. If it is baked leave it in the oven for about an hour at 200°C. When the eggplant is sufficiently cool pull off the skin and get rid of the stalk. Put the flesh, lemon juice, crushed garlic and sesame paste into a blender. Keep tasting until you have found the flavour you like. You may need more lemon juice, more garlic or even a little water to make it less thick. The consistency should be like uncooked sponge-cake mixture. When you have it right turn it out on to a flat plate and sprinkle with chopped parsley and pour a little olive oil over the entire dish. M'Tabl is ideal eaten, when it is still slightly warm, with hot Arabic bread.

Hot Buttered Cinnamon Rolls and Coffee

Buy the best cinnamon rolls you can find and heat them until the sugar topping bubbles. Make some freshly roasted coffee, and serve with foaming hot milk, topped with a melting marshmallow. Provide unsalted butter for the rolls, and warm, unscented towels to clean fingers and mouths afterwards. Have ready a bowl of fresh fruit to clear the palate.

Caviare Rolls

a tiny tin of caviare (or the ubiquitous black lumpfish roe)
four slices of the best smoked salmon, each divided into two pieces
a squeeze of lemon
black pepper
sprigs of parsley
thinly sliced brown bread and butter

Place a teaspoon of caviare into each piece of smoked salmon, add a squeeze of lemon juice and roll it up like a cigar. Repeat until you have eight caviare rolls. Garnish them with a little freshly ground black pepper and a few sprigs of parsley. Serve on one plate with the bread and butter. Do not reveal what is inside the smoked salmon and just let your partner's taste buds revel in your extravagance. Serve with white wine.

Scrambled Eggs with Smoked Salmon

4 large eggs
a dash of cream
pepper and salt
a large knob of butter
a few slivers of smoked salmon
soft toast (made with fresh bread and cooked till it is barely beige)

Beat the eggs and cream with the seasoning. Melt the butter in a non-stick saucepan and tip in the egg mixture. Cook gently, stirring all the time, until just beginning to set. Remove from the heat. Remember, scrambled eggs continue to cook even when they are nowhere near the stove. Serve on warmed plates accompanied by triangles of soft toast. Scatter with pieces of thinly sliced smoked salmon, and finish off with a little freshly ground black pepper. Serve with garden wine or champagne.

Kadin Gobegi (Ladies' Navels)

These are worth serving simply for their name, although they are most delicious to eat.

To make about one dozen fritters:

Syrup:
1 cup sugar
1 cup water
dash of fresh lemon juice

Fritters:
scant cup water
2 tablespoons butter
little salt
1 cup self-raising flour
2 eggs
oil for frying
a little almond essence
stiffly whipped cream

Combine the sugar, water and lemon juice in a saucepan and boil, stirring until sugar dissolves. Turn the heat up and continue to cook for about five minutes or until the syrup becomes thick and sticky. Remove from heat and leave to cool.

Boil the water, butter and salt in a four-pint saucepan until the butter melts. Pour in the flour all at once and beat furiously until the mixture is blended (a wooden spoon is best). It will become a doughy, stodgy mass. Beat the eggs one by one into the paste. It will gradually become smooth and shiny. Heat three or four inches of vegetable oil in a deep fryer until it becomes very hot. Take an inch or so of dough, roll it into a ball, dip your finger into the almond essence and gently press into the centre of the ball. Repeat until you have as many fritters as will easily cook at the same time. Deep fry them for about ten minutes or until they turn golden. Once they are cooked, remove and dip them into the cooled syrup. Let them cool down to lukewarm on a serving plate. Just before you take them upstairs put a dab of chilled whipped cream into the navel (i.e. depression) of the fritter.

Immam 'Bayildi (and the Imam 'Fainted)

It is pointless to make this dish for two people to finish at a single meal because it is too delicious, and small quantities look too mean. Make it for four and if the two of you finish it all do not say a word.

2 medium-sized eggplants
salt
4 onions sliced into rings
3 ripe tomatoes, chopped and de-seeded
fresh basil
olive oil
3 large cloves of garlic
black pepper
parsley

Cut off the stalks and cut the eggplants lengthwise into halves. Peel them in strips leaving the skin nearly intact. Slash the cut side several times, making inch-long cuts. Sprinkle generously with salt and arrange in a flat dish. Cover with cold water, place a heavy weight on top and leave them for a good half hour. Meanwhile combine onions, chopped tomatoes and about a teaspoon of salt in a bowl with a little fresh basil. Drain the eggplants, dry them thoroughly and heat two tablespoons of olive oil in a pan. Place the eggplants in the pan cut side up and stuff as much of the tomato/onion mixture into the slashes as possible. Pile the rest on top. Add half a clove of garlic peeled, and sprinkle liberally with about three tablespoons of olive oil. Pour in a cup of water and boil. After the dish has boiled for a couple of minutes reduce the heat and let it simmer in the covered pan for an hour or until the eggplants are tender. Allow the dish to cool to room temperature and garnish with freshly ground black pepper and parsley. Serve with chunks of Greek sesame bread or lightly toasted flat Arabic bread.

(It is worth remembering that every ingredient in this dish is considered to have aphrodisiac properties, so far unproven.)

Hummus

This recipe is the same as M'Tabl, except that half a can of prepared hummus (chick pea purée) is substituted for the eggplant. Hummus can be garnished with a little paprika and parsley along with the olive oil.

It is quite smart to provide bowls of fresh parsley after almost any Middle Eastern dish, because they almost all feature a great deal of garlic. Fresh garlic on the breath is sexy and nice, but when it is stale it is less attractive. Chewing fresh parsley not only alleviates the problem, but is a pleasant, sociable thing to do.

On Judging Beds by Their Covers

Rule 1. No double bed of any note would be seen dead in
      (a) CANDLEWICK
      (b) LILAC NET

Bedroom designed for the Paris Exhibition in 1937 by Christopher Heal:
Heal & Son Ltd. CoID PHOTOGRAPH

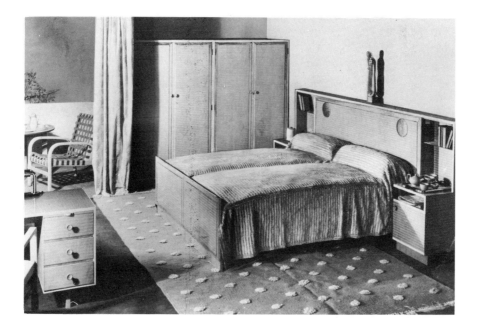

Overleaf:
The Wheel of Life, a nineteenth-century Tibetan quilt: VICTORIA AND ALBERT
MUSEUM, LONDON

IDEAL COVERS RATED ON A STAR SYSTEM:

 ☆☆☆☆☆☆☆

Original French sixteenth-century tapestry quilt which has never passed out of the family's hands. Preferably once covered Elizabeth I and is still used by family when her descendant comes to stay.

☆☆☆☆☆☆☆

Tattered lace bedspread, handmade by wretched peasants 100 years ago. Preferably beige with age and once a favourite of Lady Caroline Lamb (or some equally romantic figure) who was a great friend of the family.

☆☆☆☆☆☆

Heavy silk quilted bedspread with own petticoats. Must be rusty with age around the hem and have been in the family at least 200 years.

☆☆☆☆☆

Extremely complicated patchwork pattern quilt, stitched by brave American wives of the West as they waited in the fort for the Indians to come
OR
Quite simple patchwork pattern quilt, sewn by brave wives of the West but with original arrow holes made after Indians came.

☆☆☆☆

Modern silk/polyester or linen mix or equivalent bedspread made to fit bed precisely and matching curtains in some small details. (Nowadays such beds are seen bedecked with a great many cushions. It is extremely important that none of the cushions should match each other or anything in the room.)

☆☆☆

DUVETS Virtually unknown in America where their nearest equivalent is a 'comforter', duvets, (huge quilts filled with anything from the finest white goosedown through horse and cattle tail hair to terylene for poor allergics) have been responsible for a bedtime revolution in Britain and in Australia (where they are known as 'doonas') because they make sheets and blankets obsolete.

There was a time when no double bed worthy of the title would allow a duvet in the same room but times have changed and even the stateliest beds on show in the stateliest homes often have a duvet hidden under the aged tapestry cover. Most popular in upwardly mobile households where husbands are expected to make the bed too and therefore swear by them in the morning and at them in the evening when they favour her side of the bed.

Least popular in working-class families where easing the work burden is seen as devilish practice akin to dish-washing machines and waste disposals.

☆☆

A frightfully interesting ethnic rug a friend picked up in one of the backstreet markets for virtually nothing. Invariably 'frightfully interesting' becomes very boring after short acquaintance and ethnic rugs have bugs.

☆

An animal skin from a real animal. A terrible mistake on two counts.

(1) So many people are allergic to fur and an agreeable bedtime companion could turn into a sneezing, weeping wreck within moments.

(2) Sensitive souls don't go for animal skins any more, no matter how many times you may say it died of natural causes. Muttering that fur covers are seen on beautiful animals and ugly on beds a charming partner could disappear from your life and your bed before your very eyes.

NOTE: If there really is no other choice except the candlewick or the net dye it black, and say someone famous died. Some may find this macabre enough to excuse even candlewick.

Oak bedstead with bulbs and Corinthian capitals on the posts and the headboard carved with the arms of James I, the badge of Henry, Prince of Wales and the arms of Fredrick, Count Palatine of the Rhine, Montacute House, Somerset: THE TIMES

The Very Nearly Final Resting Place

'I'd rather be shot by a gun than stabbed with a knife but most of all I'd rather go to bed and wake up dead.'

SIX-YEAR-OLD BOY IN LONDON PLAYGROUND

EVERYONE DIES; NO ONE is spared; and the very least we can hope for is a gentle passing away without violence, disgrace or pain. Yet somehow the presence of death brings out the underlying seriousness in us and makes us very solemn and very earnest. Obviously it is all deeply rooted in a fear of the unknown and the ignominy of just dying. As the world prizefighter Joe Louis said, simply and without pretension, 'Everybody wants to go to heaven but nobody wants to die.' Even the American humorist Woody Allen – who can be extremely funny about death, 'On the plus side death is one of the few things that can be done as easily lying down' – reveals his own fears: 'I don't want to achieve immortality through my work. I want to achieve it by not dying.' His contemporary, movie-maker Mel Brooks finds death some kind of a godly con trick:

Why do we have to die? As a kid you get nice white shoes with white laces and a velvet suit with short pants and a nice collar and you go to college and you meet a nice girl and get married, work a few years and then you have to die! What is that shit? They never wrote that in the contract!

If death is inevitable, and despite the agitations of Allen and Brooks that seems irrefutable, then no one wants to die unnoticed, a forgotten heap of bedclothes on a divan in the corner. Some choose to die with a smile on their lips and a witticism to be recorded for posterity. Others wish to embrace a god they crossed the street to avoid while living. But all of us should have the chance to do our dying in peace, and from a suitable deathbed.

It is interesting, however, to see how the vital elements of good timing and luck play just as great a part in death as in life. Poor Francis Bacon, who is generally only remembered for being the man who might have written Shakespeare's plays, and equally might not have done any such thing, suffered an uninspired and uncalled-for death. His friend and companion Thomas Hobbes described the event to the essayist John Aubrey. Apparently Sir Francis had nothing wrong with him at all when he took to his carriage one snowy day in the harsh winter of 1626, but he caught a chill and so called into the house of the Earl of Arundel at Highgate where they 'put him in a good bed warmed with a pan but it was a damp bed that had not been lain in about a year before, which gave him such a cold that in two or three days he died of suffocation'.

Death was, of course, his fate, but the event should not have taken place in some damp spare bed. A deathbed should be one of substance, a bed that could tell a story or two. 'To die,' Peter Pan said, 'would be an awfully good adventure.' That may be going too far but at least it should have a certain grandeur. Lord Marchmain, the demanding, impossible patriarch created by Evelyn Waugh in *Brideshead Revisited*, insisted on dying as he had lived – in style. He came home to England to die and demanded a deathbed of truly regal splendour:

It came down the main staircase in pieces, at intervals, during the afternoon; huge sections of rococo, velvet-covered cornice; the twisted gilt and velvet columns which formed its posts; beams of unpolished

*wood, made not to be seen which performed invisible, structural
functions below the draperies; plumes of dyed feathers, which sprang
from gold-mounted ostrich eggs and crowned the canopy; finally the
mattresses with four toiling men to each corner. Lord Marchmain
seemed to derive comfort from the consequences of his whim; he sat
by the fire watching the bustle, while we stood in a half circle – Cara,
Cordelia and I – and talked to him.*

Some may consider Lord Marchmain's, and consequently his creator
Evelyn Waugh's, preoccupation with death and its trappings somewhat
morbid. But why? Surrounding death with ritual and pomp puts it
properly in its place. Once we can shroud this thing we still do not trust or
understand in intangible objects like draperies and black-edged writing
paper, we can handle it more easily.

At least one person had to be dressed – no matter how painful that may seem:
Conrad Nagel and Pola Negri, Bella Donna, 1923. KOBAL COLLECTION

In France in the eighteenth century such involvement with the 'accessories' of death was taken to extraordinary lengths. Liselotte, Duchess of Orleans and sister-in-law of Louis XIV, wrote fulsomely about ceremonial condolence in 1701. The then exiled King and Queen of England arrived dressed in what the duchess described as 'the strangest apparel' which consisted of black cloth and an extensive amount of ermine trimming. She was expected to receive them on a black bed, known as the mourning bed, in an entirely blackened room. 'Even the parquet was black and the windows hung with crepe.' Her forty or fifty servants were also garbed in black, and this gloom had to be reflected throughout the whole house.

Dying has never been cheap as Jessica Mitford noted, most tellingly, in *The American Way of Death* and although eighteenth-century England could hardly rival twentieth-century California for overblown excess, many families, particularly the Verneys of Claydon, used to hire out their large wardrobes of mourning equipment to their friends when the occasion arose. Nobody considered it infra-dig to hire mourning necessities and a great bed of state, not to mention 380 yards of black velvet and other sundries, were hired for a thirty-five-day mourning period at Marlborough House when the great Duke of Marlborough died in 1722. When the second Duke of Bedford died the special black bedroom furniture was hired for Southampton House and remained there for two years. In comparison, Lord Marchmain's pleasure in the setting up of a room in which to die seems quite subdued, but there is no doubt that the hustle and bustle of his 'arrangements' made him quite perky.

It was dark before the bed was finished; we went to see it, Lord Marchmain stepping quite briskly now through the intervening rooms. 'I congratulate you. It really looks remarkably well. Wilcox, I seem to remember a silver basin and ewer – they stood in a room we called "The Cardinal's Dressing-room". I think – suppose we had them here on the console. Then if you will send Plender and Gaston to me, the luggage can wait until tomorrow – simply the dressing case and what I need for the night. Plender will know. If you will leave me with Plender and Gaston I will go to bed. We will meet later; you will dine

here and keep me amused.' We turned to go; as I was at the door he
called me back.

> *'It looks well, does it not?'*
> *'Very well.'*
> *'You might paint it, eh – and call it "The Deathbed".'*

Lord Marchmain was certainly not alone in his positive enjoyment of getting the 'deathbed' scene right. The poet Alexander Pope wrote disapprovingly of his contemporary Sir Geoffrey Kneller:

> *I paid Sir Geoffrey Kneller a visit but two days before he died. I think I never saw a scene of so much vanity in my life. He was lying in his bed, and contemplating the plan he had made for his monument. He said many gross things in relation to himself and the memory he should leave behind him. He said he should not like to lie among the rascals at Westminster; a memorial there would be sufficient; and desired me to write an epitaph for it. I did so afterwards and I think it's the worst thing I ever wrote in my life.*

Other worthier souls spent the time on their deathbeds more profitably than in the devising of monuments. Florence Nightingale was advised by her consultant to take to her bed in 1857 and not rise from it for the rest of her life. To everyone's amazement she did as she was told for once and retired to her 'deathbed' where she remained for fifty-three years. Far from being a mournful, gloomy sort of place in the Victorian tradition, Florence Nightingale's deathbed was a positive hive of activity. She toiled away mercilessly, establishing training schools for nurses and midwives, advising the government on India even though she'd never set foot there, and killing off one Minister of the Crown, Sidney Herbert, and one poet, Arthur Hugh Clough, with overwork. She never truly believed that those who slaved for her prodigiously over the years could possibly let her down by dying and refused to believe that Sidney Herbert, who had loved and admired her all his life, was ill. Two months before he died in 1861 she wrote: 'I believe you have many years of usefulness before you.' She herself outlived him by forty-nine years. Finally as a blind old lady she played out her own deathbed scene. None of her contemporaries or allies was there to mourn her. She had outlived them all. She refused to be buried in Westminster Abbey, not because the place was full of the rascals to whom Sir Geoffrey Kneller had objected, but because she felt herself unworthy. She was laid to rest in the family graveyard under a small stone reading: 'F.N. Born 1820. Died 1910.'

Perhaps one of the most stylish deathbed scenes was accomplished by Honoré Gabriel Victor Riquetti, Comte de Mirabeau who was one of the great historical figures of the French Revolution. Just days before his death in 1791 he had been chatting to his friend Comte la Marck, who said that in his view the most beautiful and impressive deaths he had seen – and there had been many – had been accomplished by those who requested nothing more than to be placed in such a position as to enable them to pass away with as little suffering as possible. When his time came Mirabeau asked the count, who was at his side, to arrange him suitably, and then said with a sigh: 'And now, connoisseur in beautiful deaths, are you satisfied?'

His very last moments were recorded by P.J.G. Cabanis, who was there:

> As soon as day dawned he ordered the windows to be thrown open and said to me, with a firm voice and a calm tone: 'My friend, I shall die today. When one has come so far there is only one thing left to do; to perfume oneself, to crown oneself with flowers and to surround oneself with beautiful music in order to enter agreeably into that sleep from which there is no awakening.'

Opposite: top
'Death Helping an Old Lover into Bed' by Thomas Rowlandson: HENRY E. HUNTINGTON LIBRARY AND ART GALLERY

Opposite: bottom
'The Miser's End' by Thomas Rowlandson: HENRY E. HUNTINGTON LIBRARY AND ART GALLERY

133

The artist William Blake (1757–1827) was another who took pleasure in dying. He ended his days singing great Hallelujahs and songs of joy and triumph. The account of his death, written by his good friend, Frederick Tatham, goes into great descriptive detail: 'He sang loudly and with true ecstatic energy and seemed too happy that he had finished his course, that he had run his race.' But the great man had not forgotten, in his orgy of hymn singing, the needs of his splendid and faithful wife. Tatham went on to note that:

having answered a few questions concerning his wife's means of living after his decease . . . his spirit departed like the sighing of a gentle breeze and he slept in company with the mighty ancestors he had formerly depicted . . . such was the entertainment of the last hours of his life. It was prelude to the hymns of saints. It was an overture to the choir of heaven. It was a chant to the response of angels.

'Dying was once a public process in the life of the individual and a most exemplary one; think of the medieval pictures in which the deathbed has turned into a throne toward which the people press through the wide-open doors of the death house. In the course of modern times dying has been pushed further and further out of the perceptual world of the living. There used to be no house, hardly a room, in which someone had not once died. Today people live in rooms that have never been touched by death, dry dwellers of eternity, and when their end approaches they are stowed away in sanatoria or hospitals by their heirs. It is, however, characteristic that not only a man's knowledge or wisdom, but above all his real life first assumes transmissible form at the moment of his death. Just as a sequence of images is set in motion inside a man as his life comes to an end – unfolding the views of himself under which he has encountered himself without being aware of it – suddenly in his expression and looks the unforgettable emerges and imparts to everything that concerned him that authority which even the poorest wretch in dying possesses for the living around him.

(WALTER BENJAMIN)

The poet William Carlos Williams, who died in 1963 aged eighty, was not one who rejoiced in death but he would, I think, have approved of the dignity of the Mirabeau way of death. Just before he died he wrote: 'It astonishes me to observe how irritated moderns become, not so much at the thought as at the mention of death. That's one thing they don't know how to take. I don't mean that we should be "brave". That stinks. But it is equally asinine to pretend to ignore it.' G. B. Shaw, naturally, went further: 'Life does not cease to be funny when people die any more than it ceases to be serious when people laugh.' (*Doctor's Dilemma*).

Perhaps the best way of warding off our subconscious fears of death and what may or may not be waiting for us on 'the other side' is in collecting quotable deathbed sayings. I cannot help having doubts about their being genuine last words, because who can time his or her own death to match the best quote? Who would not be tempted, having dropped the '*mot juste*', to improve, extemporize and then ruin the whole thing? But as we, the living, have no way of knowing, or even guessing about such matters, we can only accept famous last words at their face value and

No one died quite like Greta Garbo: <u>Camille</u>, 1936. Kobal Collection

simply enjoy their wit, their humour and their excellent timing. Nancy Astor, who died in 1964, upon seeing the family group assembled around her deathbed said: 'Am I dying or is this my birthday?'

The Reverend Sidney Smith, who was genuinely funny all of his life, did not let the side down on his deathbed. Upon being told that he had sipped from an ink-well instead of his medicine bottle he cried: 'Then bring me all the blotting paper in the house.'

David Garrick's canopied bed, *c.* 1775: Victoria and Albert Museum, London.
CoID PHOTOGRAPH

We are invited to take our choice over Beethoven's dying words. One version is 'I shall hear in heaven', which sentimental musicians would probably prefer. The other is: 'Applaud friends, the comedy is over.' I am inclined to go with version one simply because version two had already been spoken – at least twice and long before Beethoven's death in 1827. The Greek philosopher Demonax, who died in 150 BC, is reputed to have said, 'Draw the curtain, the farce is over.' Some time later, in 1553, the French writer, François Rabelais is purported to have said an almost identical 'Ring down the curtain, the farce is over.' Some who refuse to believe that such a great man as Rabelais could possibly be accused of plagiarism, maintain the Greek before him had said 'the *fuss* is over', referring to Hellenic politics of the time, but as he presumably spoke in Classical Greek, in which the words for 'fuss' and 'farce' are *fussaria* and *kōmōidia*, such confusion seems unlikely.

Perhaps some of the most charming and memorable last words are those that reveal more concern for worried friends and relations than the fact of imminent death. Lady Emerald Cunard, who died in 1948 having been a devoted socialite all her life and never noted for generosity or solicitude towards her staff said as she declined a teaspoon of champagne: 'No. Open a bottle for the nurse and for yourself.'

Henry Fox, the first Baron Holland, on his death in 1774 said: 'If Mr Selwyn calls again show him up. If I am alive I shall be delighted to see him and if I am dead he would like to see me.'

Mrs David Garrick, wife of the great actor and a tartar all her life, saw no reason why she should change her tune, dying or not, and her last words were as a maid offered her a cup of tea: 'Put it down hussy. Do you think I cannot help myself?'

I find Rudolph Valentino's last words very moving in their innocence and utter lack of awareness that death was waiting: 'Don't pull down the blinds. I feel fine. I want the sunlight to greet me.'

Daniel Defoe, in 1731, was only concerned with the importance of dying as an Englishman should, with no fuss. 'I do not know which is more difficult in a Christian life – to live well or to die well.'

A very different Englishman, W. Somerset Maugham, said in 1965: 'Dying is a very dull, dreary affair and my advice to you is to have nothing to do with it.'

There are many sets of famous last words attributed to Oscar Wilde

'Death of Voltaire': English painted wax by Samuel Percy, VICTORIA AND ALBERT MUSEUM, LONDON

and it is perfectly reasonable to accept that he said them all, letting one deathless quote follow the other as death itself kept him waiting. My favourite, however, is his complaint when he turned over in his bed with his face to the wall: 'This wallpaper is killing me. One of us will have to go.'

It is tempting to hope that the last words of a favourite writer, artist or human being will show magnanimity, generosity or at the very least the wit that made them famous in their lifetime. Often we are well rewarded, as with W. C. Fields, who said, referring to his least favourite city: 'On the whole, I'd rather be in Philadelphia.' The opera singer Kathleen Ferrier showed spunk with: 'Now I'll have *eine kleine* pause.' But Dorothy Parker, who has always been my own favourite humorist and observer of life let me down terribly with her last words, revealing that beneath the biting wit was an insecure, lonely soul who wanted desperately to be liked – just like everybody else. She actually died alone in 1967 with no one to record the very final words, if there were any, but her last sentence to her friend Beatrice Ames was a querulous one. 'I want you to tell me the truth. Did Ernest (Hemingway) really like me?'

If famous last words can be called the epitaphs of the very nearly final resting place then it is fitting that this book should end with an epitaph; not one composed by others about a famous or infamous personality but one written in advance by the subject, in the hope that his fellow beings would find it agreeable. Such an epitaph was written by Benjamin Franklin when he was twenty-five and reflects without undue sentimentality or self-righteousness a healthy belief in the hereafter.

The body of Ben Franklin, printer, (like the cover of an old book, its contents torn out and stripped of its lettering and gilding) lies here, food for worms. But the work shall not be lost, for it will (as he believed) appear in a new and more elegant edition revised and corrected by the author.

LAST WORDS

'I must sleep now.' (LORD BYRON)

'I have been a most unconscionable time a-dying, but I hope you will
excuse it.' (CHARLES II)

'Nurse, it was I who discovered that leeches have red blood.'
(CUVIER, TO THE NURSE WHO WAS APPLYING LEECHES)

'I suffer nothing, but I feel a sort of difficulty in living longer.'
(FONTENELLE)

'We are all going to heaven and Van Dyck is of the company.'
(GAINSBOROUGH)

'So here it is at last, the distinguished thing.' (HENRY JAMES)

'Hold your tongue! Your wretched chatter disgusts me.'
(MALESHERBES, TO THE PRIEST)

'I see no reason why the existence of Harriet Martineau should be
perpetuated.' (HARRIET MARTINEAU)

'Crito, I owe a cock to Aesculapius.' (SOCRATES)

'I'll be shot if I don't believe I'm dying.' (LORD THURLOW)

Sandra Harris was born and brought up in Perth, Australia. She came to Britain in 1964 and joined the BBC, working on the news and current affairs programme, 'The World at One', and also doing various radio specials. In 1969 she joined Thames Television's 'Today' programme with Eamonn Andrews, and worked on that and other projects through the seventies. In 1975 she co-presented the late-night chat show 'Take Two', with Llew Gardner. In 1978 she started her own programme, 'People in the News', once referred to as London's first TV gossip column. The programme later became 'Sandra' and was devoted to coverage of theatre and film events in London. In July 1981 she left Thames to write her first book, **The Nice Girl's Handbook**, and to work on various freelance projects. She lives in London with her Palestinian husband and three children.